OUR WORLD

THE PEOPLE'S REPUBLIC OF CHINA

by MARGARET RAU

Illustrated with photographs

JULIAN MESSNER   NEW YORK

Published by Julian Messner, a Division of Simon & Schuster, Inc.
1 West 39 Street, New York, N.Y. 10018. All rights reserved.

Printed in the United States of America
Design by Marjorie Zaum

To my good friends—
Rémi, Norbert, and Yves Tan

BOOKS BY MARGARET RAU
Our World: The People's Republic of China
The Yangtze River
The Yellow River
Jimmy of Cherry Valley

Library of Congress Cataloging in Publication Data

Rau, Margaret.
    Our world: the People's Republic of China.

    SUMMARY: An introduction to the third largest
country in the world emphasizing the way of life of the people.
    1. China—Juvenile literature. [1. China]
I. Title.

DS706.R38   1974   915.1'03'5   73-19237
ISBN 0-671-32639-2
ISBN 0-671-32640-6 (lib. bdg.)

Students of the Yuping No. 2 Middle School, Shanghai, play together in ▶
table-tennis games.

Contents

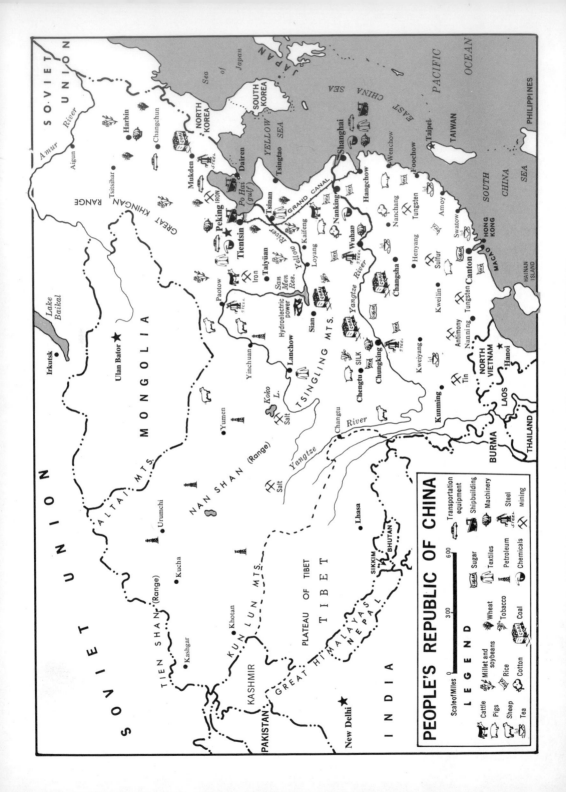

PEOPLE'S REPUBLIC OF CHINA

LEGEND

Scale of Miles
0   300   600

Cattle	Millet and soybeans
Pigs	Wheat
Sheep	Rice
Tea	Cotton

Sugar	Textiles
	Tobacco
	Coal

Transportation equipment	Shipbuilding
	Machinery
	Steel
	Mining
Petroleum	Chemicals

SOVIET UNION

MONGOLIA

Ulan Bator

Lake Baikal

Irkutsk

Amur River

Aigun

Tsitsihar

Harbin

Changchun

GREAT KHINGAN RANGE

Mukden

Dairen

NORTH KOREA

SOUTH KOREA

Sea of Japan

JAPAN

YELLOW SEA

Tsingtao

Tsinan

Peking

Tientsin

Po Hai (gulf)

IRON

COAL STEEL

Taiyüan

Iron

Paotow

STEEL

Yinchuan

Yellow River

Kaifeng

Loyang

San Men Res.

Hydroelectric Power

Sian

Lanchow

TSINGLING MTS.

Yumen

Koko L.
Salt

NAN SHAN (Range)

Salt

Yangtze

Changtu River

Chengtu

SILK

Chungking

STEEL

Kunming

Yangtze River

Wuhan

COAL STEEL

Nanking

Hangchow

Shanghai

Wenchow

Nanchang

Tungsten

Changsha

Henyang

Sulfur

Hengyang

Kweilin

Antimony

Kweiyang

Tin

Nanning

Tungsten

Canton

HONG KONG

MACAO

Foochow

Swatow

Amoy

SOUTH CHINA SEA

Taipei

TAIWAN

HAINAN ISLAND

EAST CHINA SEA

PACIFIC OCEAN

PHILIPPINES

GRAND CANAL

TIEN SHAN (Range)

Urumchi

Kucha

Kashgar

Khotan

KUN LUN MTS.

PLATEAU OF TIBET

TIBET

Lhasa

GREAT HIMALAYAS

NEPAL

SIKKIM

BHUTAN

KASHMIR

PAKISTAN

INDIA

New Delhi

BURMA

LAOS

THAILAND

NORTH VIETNAM

Hanoi

ALTAI MTS.

SOUTH CHINA SEA

 **1**

Victory at
the United Nations

In the autumn of 1971, a heated debate was going on in the huge General Assembly hall in the United Nations building in New York. Every year for twenty years, there had been the same debate—should the People's Republic of China be admitted to the United Nations? For twenty years the vote had been "no."

The question came up because, in 1949, the army of the Chinese Communist Party had overthrown the Nationalist Government of China. Chiang Kai-shek, the Nationalist leader, and his army had retreated to Taiwan, an island off the South China coast. There he set up his own government, while on the mainland, the Communists founded the People's Republic of China. So there were two Chinese governments. But since Chiang Kai-shek was still recognized as the legitimate ruler of China, he continued to send his own delegation to the United Nations. This action caused a difference of opinion among member UN countries.

The Soviet Union and the Communist countries of Eastern Europe insisted that the delegation should rightfully come from the People's Republic. However, almost all of the nations from the Western world voted for the delegation from Taiwan. They believed that the new Communist nation

on the Asian mainland would collapse and that the Nationalists would return to power again.

As time went by, however, it became obvious that the
People's Republic of China was firmly established. And so
each fall, when the question of Communist China's admission came up, she began to receive more votes—although
not enough to win.

In 1971, when the subject was being discussed once again,
there was a difference. The United States still backed her old
ally, Chiang Kai-shek. But this time she was ready to accept
two Chinese delegations—one from the People's Republic
and the other from the Nationalist government.

Then things really began to happen. The little country of
Albania, which was the strongest ally of the People's Republic
of China, asked for a speedy vote to expel the Nationalist
delegation and seat the Communist one.

George Bush, the United States Ambassador to the United
Nations, tried to gain more time by asking that the expulsion
of Taiwan be made an important question. (An important
question always has to be passed by a two-thirds vote.) The
United States was sure she could get enough votes at least
to keep the Nationalist government from being expelled.

One debate followed another, and it was plain that some
of the delegations disagreed with the United States. Finally
the Assembly voted on Bush's motion and defeated it, 59
to 55. The delegation from Taiwan stalked out of the Assembly hall, realizing that they would be expelled.

Now the vote was taken on Albania's motion. When it
was over, it was 76 to 35 in favor of seating the delegation
from the People's Republic of China. At last China's great
mainland, which is second only to Russia in size and contains

one fourth of the world's population, was going to be represented in the United Nations.

For twenty years, Communist China had been shut away from the rest of the world. Now, perhaps, the Western world would have an opportunity to learn more about the country and its people.

 **2**

An Ancient Civilization

China's very long history has often been told through its dynasties, or royal families. For 3,500 years, these dynasties swept over China like the waves of the sea. Each one would establish a new empire, reach a peak of glory and splendor, and then weaken and be overthrown. A new dynasty would rise in its place.

The men who founded the dynasties came from all walks of life. Some were peasants, others were military officers, and still others were invading chieftains from the nomad countries of Mongolia, Manchuria, and Tibet. When a dynasty was at its height of power, the Emperor held lavish court and received rich tribute from as far away as India, Arabia, and Persia. It was easy for the Chinese to believe that their country, which they called the Middle Kingdom, was at the center of everything and that their Emperor was the Son of Heaven.

As the Son of Heaven, chosen by Heaven itself to rule, the Emperor held solemn rituals in sacred temples. There he prayed for peace, prosperity, and rain to ensure good harvests.

China was a nation of farmers, and the welfare of the whole Empire rested on the success or failure of the crops. So any true history of China must concern itself with the peasant farmers.

Millions of peasants lived in cramped huts throughout the countryside. They worked in the fields from the time they were able to walk until they died. But no matter how long they worked, they often went hungry because of the high taxes placed on them by the Emperor.

The tax collectors took not only grain but also vegetables, oil, pigs, chickens, fish, and fruit. All of this enabled the Emperor and his court to live in splendor and plenty. Even when droughts and floods brought lean seasons, there were always full granaries for the Emperor.

But the peasants were continually faced with famine. Millions died, and the roadsides were lined with bodies bloated by the grass, tree bark, and earth they had eaten to ward off hunger.

Good weather conditions meant the difference between life and death to the peasants. So they worshipped thousands of gods who, they believed, controlled nature. There was the god of thunder, the god of rain, the god of good harvest and the Father of Heaven and the Mother of Earth.

Images of the gods stood in tiny wayside shrines overlooking the fields. On their way to work at dawn, and on their

After work was done, peasants worshipped at wayside shrines.

way home at dusk, the peasants stopped to burn incense and pray for help from the gods. As the centuries passed, this ancient nature worship became a religion called Taoism, with elaborate temples and priests.

Daily life for the peasants was hard enough, but they were also used by the emperors for many other purposes. In times of war, they became beasts of burden to carry the soldiers' supplies. When great projects were built, the peasants did the work. With primitive tools, they dug the canals and built the imperial highways and palaces.

The biggest of these projects was the Great Wall, which was begun by Chin Shih Huang Ti, first emperor of China, who ruled from 221 to 207 B.C. Chin Shih Huang Ti sent millions of peasants to the wild mountains and cold plains that lay between Mongolia and Manchuria and China. He ordered the peasants to build a wall high enough and strong enough to keep out the fierce northern tribesmen, who were enemies of the Chinese.

Much of the wall had to be built on mountains so steep that it was difficult to find footing. Yet sweating, straining men worked from dawn to dark, carrying huge rocks up the sides of these mountains to build two parallel walls along the summits. The walls were 21 feet apart, and long lines of men lugged heavy baskets of earth up the mountains and dumped it between the walls. Thousands of other men, using heavy wooden mallets, tamped the earth into a hard filling.

Working conditions were miserable. The men froze in winter and roasted in summer. Their only food was a watery gruel. When they weakened, they were beaten by overseers until they dropped. Those who died—and there were many— were flung between the walls and tamped down with the

China's ancient Great Wall.

earth. For many years the Chinese called the wall, which is about 1,500 miles long, the Great Burial Wall.

Though the Chinese peasants are known for their patience, they have always rebelled when conditions became too unbearable. And so they rose up against the Chin Dynasty. They were led by a peasant, Kao-tzu, who founded the Han Dynasty.

Much as the peasants endured under the emperors, they suffered even more whenever the dynasties fell apart. Then the wild tribes from Mongolia, Manchuria, and Tibet invaded China. These fierce nomadic peoples spent most of their time astride horses, herding their cattle from place to place over the wide treeless plains of the cold north. They hated fields and villages, for this was not their way of life. So they turned their cattle loose on the peasants' fields, burned the villages, killed the men, and carried off the women and children to be their slaves.

During the Mongol invasions of the second and third centuries A.D., Buddhism was brought to China and spread rapidly among the peasants. Buddhism, which was begun in the sixth century B.C. by a rich young Indian nobleman, Siddhartha Gautama, taught that people are born not once but many times. If you lived a life of good deeds, your next life would be a good one. If you lived a life of evil, your next one would be full of misfortune. This was called the law of karma. When you had paid all your karma, you would enter eternal bliss and be done with suffering. And so the peasants thought that if they bore everything patiently, as Buddhism taught, their next life would be a good one.

Sometimes emperors and empresses, noblemen and scholars became Buddhists. But they were more likely to follow the philosophy known as Confucianism, named for its founder, Kung Fu-tse, or Confucius.

Confucius, a scholar himself, lived from 551 to 479 B.C. He taught such simple morals as: "The people should obey their ruler, but the ruler should act like a father to his people" and "Learning without thinking is labor lost; thinking without learning is perilous."

While he lived Confucius was not given much attention. But after his death, scholars began to take more and more notice of his works. They wrote long explanations of his simple sayings, and soon these explanations grew into big volumes. To be a scholar, you had to know the contents of these volumes. If you had memorized them well enough to pass the examinations that were given by the Imperial Academy, you could become a court official. Officials exchanged their tunics and trousers for long ceremonial robes and elaborate hats, which they wore when attending the emperor's court.

Almost all the emperors chose Confucian scholars to help them run the government. Because of the power they held through their learning, the scholar class was revered. In theory anyone, even a peasant, could become a scholar, pass the examinations, and be appointed a court official. But actually it was almost impossible for a peasant's son to find the time or opportunity to do the necessary studying. Usually only the sons of noblemen or wealthy landowners became officials, and they used their power to pass laws that would benefit their own class.

Confucianism taught that the family was the most important unit in society. And in China, the family meant far more than mother and father and children. It included grandfather and grandmother, uncles, aunts and cousins, all living together in one household.

Grandfather was in charge of the family's business affairs. Grandmother ruled the home. No matter how old the children were, they still obeyed their parents. Each one also obeyed all the members of the family who were older than he.

Families not only revered their living relatives, but also honored their ancestors. They took care of their graves, and set up red-lacquered memorial tablets in the family ancestral hall. In a solemn ceremony each New Year's season, all the relatives gathered in the hall to honor their dead.

Ancestral worship made life very difficult for young brides. Parents chose the mates for their children, often when they were just babies. And the young couple saw each other for the first time at the wedding.

Afterwards, the bride went to live with her mother-in-law and her husband's relatives. To gain respect in the new household, she had to bear a son, because only a son could carry on the ancestral worship. Until that son was born, the young wife was treated harshly, especially by her mother-in-law. The worst misfortune that could befall her was to bear a succession of girls.

Girls had little importance in China. An old Chinese proverb expresses the general attitude toward them: "A woman's humanity is as worthless as a coward's bravery."

In times of great poverty, female children of peasants were either abandoned to die or were sold into families to become second wives. Such wives were called concubines, but they were treated like slaves. Almost every wealthy man in China had several concubines, and the emperors had hundreds of them.

In the families of the rich, girls were kept secluded at home. Though they were sometimes taught to read and write, most of their education was concerned with how to run a household. Above all, they were schooled in obedience.

One of the worst tortures that young girls experienced began in A.D. 950, when tiny feet became fashionable. When girls reached the age of eight, their feet were bound in long strips of wet cloth. As the cloth dried, it would shrink and squeeze the foot. Each week, the binding was pulled tighter.

The pain was so unbearable that the girls spent most of their time crying or whimpering. Finally, when they were twelve, the bandages came off. The suffering was over, but their feet had become tiny stumps and they were hopeless cripples. If they were girls of rich families, they were carried everywhere on the backs of servants and waited on hand and foot. If they were peasant girls, they hobbled about at their work or crawled around on their knees.

Mothers grieved at having to make their daughters suffer, but they knew that, without binding their feet, it would be impossible to find them husbands. An unmarried girl was considered as much a disgrace as a young widow.

While the peasants lived a life of suffering and hardship, the lot of women was the worst of all.

 **3**

Revolution!

In 1644 the Ming Dynasty, which had ruled China for more than 250 years, was overthrown by the Manchu tribes of Manchuria under their leader, Nurhachi. Nurhachi established the Ching, or Manchu, Dynasty, the last to rule China.

Most of the Ching emperors looked to the past rather than to the future. They believed that China was still the center of the whole world, and that all other nations were barbarians who owed allegiance to the Son of Heaven.

It was a bad time for such backward views because the Western world was becoming more and more aware of China's riches. As early as the sixteenth century, Portuguese traders had sailed into Chinese coastal ports to buy tea and silk.

As time went by, the Portuguese were followed by Spanish, English, Dutch, and American trading ships. The crews on these ships were usually a drunken, brawling lot, and the Chinese despised them as "foreign devils." Believing their homelands were as barbaric as they, the Ching Emperor refused to have diplomatic relations with them. He did allow his people to trade with them, however, because trade brought money into China. But he permitted it only in the south China city of Canton.

For a while the Chinese willingly exported tea and silk, but they bought nothing in return. Their own country, they bragged, could provide them with everything they needed.

Then the British found something the Chinese wanted to buy. It was opium that came from India, one of England's Asian colonies. Opium is a narcotic drug that can be smoked in a pipe. Once a person starts using it, he becomes addicted and is unable to give it up. Opium creates a feeling of well-being, but the addict becomes listless and is unable to work. All he craves is to be allowed to smoke and dream away his life.

The Ching Emperor soon realized how harmful opium was to his subjects. He forbade the British to import it, but they ignored him. The First Opium War broke out between the two countries, and it lasted from 1839 to 1842.

China's poorly equipped soldiers were no match for the well trained British soldiers with their modern weapons. At sea the clumsy fleet of war junks was easily capsized by the British gunboats.

When the British won, they forced the Ching Emperor to sign the Treaty of Nanking. Under this treaty, the Emperor had to allow the sale of opium in China. He had to pay the costs of the war and cede the port of Hong Kong to Britain. He also had to open four more ports—Amoy, Ningpo, Foochow, and Shanghai—to foreign trade.

The British were granted the right to live in special sections of these cities and to carry on trade from them. And they could try their own citizens for any crimes committed in China. Other Western countries quickly demanded the same privileges, and the weak Ching Emperor had to grant them.

In 1856 the Second Opium War, this time involving China, England and France, resulted in the opening of more ports. France took all Indochina, which until that time had been part of the Ching Empire. And the Ching Emperor was forced to permit foreign embassies to locate in Peking.

Through the years that followed, China's situation worsened. In 1860, Russia took part of Manchuria and added it to Siberia. In 1886, the British annexed Burma. In 1895, Japan took Taiwan; fifteen years later, she annexed Korea.

The world powers were also demanding special concessions. These included deals to build railroads with money they lent to the Ching Emperor at exorbitant

On June 29, 1873 the Emperor received foreign representatives.

interest rates. The Emperor was also forced to promise protection to missionaries who wanted to run Christian schools, hospitals, and churches outside the foreign sections. And he had to allow foreigners to manage the Chinese customs office, which taxed imports and exports.

The cutting-up of China went on and on. Russia and Japan obtained leases on large pieces of land in the Liaotung Peninsula. Germany asked for and was given the same rights in Shantung Province. France got a 99-year lease on Canton. And the English invaded Tibet and sent their gunboats up and down the Yangtze River.

Finally, in 1899, John Hay, the American Secretary of State proposed the Open-Door Policy. There would be no special favors. All nations would agree to trade with China on an equal basis, and not to annex any more of her territory. They also agreed that China should keep her independence.

Although this policy kept China from being farther divided, it did not save her from the greed of foreign business concerns. China's millions of people lived on the verge of starvation, and they could be hired for very low wages to work in factories. This, plus the world-wide market for silk for which China was well known, encouraged foreigners to build silk factories. Shanghai was the logical city for such factories. Standing on the Whangpoo River, which flows into the mouth of the Yangtze River, it is in the very center of a large silkworm-producing area.

Starving peasants began flocking to Shanghai looking for jobs in the factories. Children as young as eight years old were employed. Standing in long rows before steaming vats in dark factory rooms, they used wooden poles to push the silkworm cocoons down into the boiling water. All day long children hovered over the vats, sweltering in the hot airless rooms, scalded now and then by the steam. They seldom got more than food and shelter for their work. The food was poor, and their shelter was only a mat spread out on the factory floor.

Adult workers weren't treated any better. They received only a few cents a day for working more than twelve hours. And they lived in a sea of hovels which surrounded the stately buildings and pleasant parks in the foreign quarter.

Epidemics of typhoid, cholera, and bubonic plague swept through the slum areas, killing thousands of workers. But there were always many more to take their place.

Whether the peasant came to the city as a laborer or tried to make ends meet in the fields, his lot was still a hopeless one. His method of work had changed very little over the centuries. Out in the fields, he toiled away with the same primitive tools his ancestors had used— wooden hoes and plows to which he sometimes harnessed himself, drawing the plow which his son guided.

Fields were irrigated with buckets of water or wooden water wheels set up on the banks of rivers or ponds. By treading on the paddles that turned the wheel, the farmer could make it revolve. Then dippers scooped up the water and dumped it into the fields.

The peasants no longer wore the graceful tunics and trousers of former centuries. Now men and women alike were clad in short, shapeless blue jackets and trousers. And instead of gathering their hair into a knot on top of the head, as had been the custom before, all the men now wore Manchu-style pigtails. The head was shaved except for a small patch on the crown, which was allowed to grow and was then braided and hung down in back.

When the Ching Dynasty had first come to power, the Emperor had ordered all Chinese men to wear this style of clothing and hair, to stamp them as Manchu subjects. If they refused, they were beheaded.

In the early days, the Chinese had hated the pigtail. But as time went by, they got used to it. By the 1800s, they were ashamed to appear without it. Even though the pigtail had become a part of their life-style, they continued to hate the Manchu officials, who were becoming more and more corrupt.

In every country village, tax collectors overcharged the peasants and pocketed the money that was to be used to repair roads and dykes (raised mud banks to keep out the river waters). During heavy rainfalls, the weak dykes often broke and floods destroyed thousands of acres of farmland. Then, once again, there would be widespread famine and death.

When times were bad, peasants borrowed money or grain from the rich landlords. If they couldn't repay their debts, the landlords took over their land and charged them high rents for working it. And if the peasants couldn't pay the rents, their children would be taken away as payment. Or the peasants would be thrown off the land. With no way of earning a living, they became beggars. Soon the country was swarming with beggars, who even formed guilds to protect themselves.

Other peasants became bandits. They joined together, hiding out in wild mountainous areas. From there, they raided farming villages in the lowlands, robbed travelers, or held them for ransom.

The patience of the peasants was again reaching the breaking point. Uprisings were becoming more and more frequent. One of the biggest of these uprisings, the Taiping Rebellion, took place in 1851.

Taiping means Heavenly Kingdom, and the movement was given that name by Hung Hsiu-chuan, the man who led it. Hung had founded a religion of his own based on the Christian religion, which he had learned from missionaries in Canton. He maintained that in a vision the Christian God, in the form of an old man, appeared to him and ordered him to save humanity.

Hung became convinced that his mission was to overthrow the Manchu. As his revolt grew, millions of unhappy peasants joined his army. The Taiping soldiers were so ferocious that the Manchu armies were no match for them. They swept up from south China, killing people and burning citics on their way. Finally they reached Nanking, which stands on the lower Yangtze. There Hung established the capital of his Heavenly Kingdom.

Hung would doubtless have succeeded in overthrowing the Ching Dynasty. But the western powers intervened because they felt they would get more concessions from the weak Ching Emperor than the independent Hung.

In 1864, thirteen years after it had begun, the rebellion was put down, and Hung committed suicide. By this time many cities and villages in southern and central China had been destroyed, and ten million people had been killed.

Then, in 1866, two years after the Taiping Rebellion had been quelled, a boy was born to the Sun family.

The Suns were considered middle-class peasants as they owned a small piece of land near their village of Choy Hang in South China.

Young Sun Yat-sen was sent to the village school by his father. He had a bright, inquisitive mind, and memorizing the ancient Confucian classics bored him. He was more interested in getting answers to questions that affected his country and its people. If China was the center of the world, why were other nations so much stronger? he asked. If the Confucian classics were supposed to train good officials, why were so many corrupt?

Sun also objected to many old customs that seemed ridiculous to him. He fought bitterly to keep his mother from binding the feet of his eight-year-old sister, but he was unsuccessful.

The Taiping Rebellion had started in Sun's part of the country, and the memory of those days was still fresh in the minds of the Manchu officials there. Mr. Sun was afraid that his young son would cause trouble for the whole family. So he sent the twelve-year-old-boy off to Hawaii to live with his older brother, Ah Mi.

Ah Mi was one of many thousands of Chinese peasants who had left to find work in foreign countries. Though many of them started out as laborers, some became wealthy businessmen.

Ah Mi was one of these. He was therefore able to send his brother to an English high school, from which the young man graduated with honors. But when Sun returned to his home village, he was full of modern ideas. His open contempt for the old-fashioned ways of doing things made the villagers call him a radical.

Once more, his father and brother decided that the best way to keep him out of trouble was to send him back to school. Young Sun studied medicine, and in 1892 he graduated from the Queen Victoria Medical College in Hong Kong. But though he was now a doctor, he was not interested in practicing medicine. He simply had wanted the degree of doctor to impress his scholar- conscious countrymen.

"I became a doctor only in order to have free access everywhere," he said later.

Sun had one goal in life—to overthrow the Manchu and establish a republic like that of the United States. He traveled throughout the world speaking for this cause. His audiences were Chinese people who had emigrated from China. Peasants themselves once, they remembered their suffering and donated large sums of money for the purchase of guns and ammunition.

Dr. Sun proved a forceful speaker, and soon the Manchus put a price of $750,000 on his head. He knew if he were caught he would be tortured until he died, just as associates of his had been.

But the knowledge of the horrible death that lay in wait for him didn't stop Dr. Sun. He continued to raise money and buy guns and ammunition, which he smuggled into China. From time to time, he himself returned secretly to the country to enlist recruits for the coming revolution. With his friends, he planned to overthrow the Manchu. But over and over, the plots were exposed and Dr. Sun would just manage to escape.

While he worked and waited, he saw the failure of one more uprising. It was started in 1900 by a secret society called the Order of the Patriotic Harmonious Fists. The West came to know this event as the Boxer Rebellion.

The Boxer Rebellion was aimed primarily at driving the foreigners out of China, but the Western armies crushed it easily. Once more a humiliated China was forced to pay damages, this time amounting to $333,000,000.

The United States, which received $23,000,000 of this sum, returned half of it to China to provide scholarships for Chinese students in American universities. As a result, many young Chinese came in close contact with the Western world. When they returned to China, they brought valuable knowledge with them.

Another result of the Boxer Rebellion was that the Empress Dowager Tzu Hsi, who was then ruling China, called for some reforms in education. Courses in natural sciences, political economy, and modern languages were now taught in Chinese schools along with the classics.

But this was not nearly enough for Dr. Sun. He continued to build up his own secret society of revolutionaries, who called themselves the Dare-to-Dies. As the years went by, they grew stronger and bolder. Some began cutting off their pigtails to show their contempt for the Manchus, even though they knew it might mean death.

Then, on October 10, 1911, the Dare-to-Dies staged an open rebellion in Hankow. The Manchu armies there either fled in terror or deserted to the rebels. The Dare-to-Dies went on to capture Nanking. And, early in 1912, they founded the new Republic of China, with Nanking as its capital. There was rejoicing all over China. And thousands of men cut off their pigtails to show that the Manchu domination was at an end.

But the Dare-to-Die army could not continue its march to the capital city of Peking. It was ruled by the Manchu general-in-chief, Yuan Shih-kai, who had seized control from the Ching Dynasty.

The leaders of the Republic tried to work with General Yuan by offering him the Presidency in place of Dr. Sun. Yuan accepted and the new republic then elected a National Assembly. The major party, which was headed by Dr. Sun, called itself the Kuomintang or Nationalist Party. The Kuomintang leaders tried to work with General Yuan, but he betrayed the Republic and made himself a dictator. The Republic was forced to move its headquarters to Canton, where Dr. Sun was named President. But he was president of a republic that had no power at all.

World War I added to the country's unrest. China joined the allies against Germany, and tens of thousands

Yuan Shih-kai reviewing his army. Note soldiers still wear the Manchu pigtail.

of Chinese laborers helped dig trenches. But after Germany's defeat, Japan boldly announced that she was going to seize German holdings in China's Shantung Province. The other allied nations, weary of war, made few objections.

Thousands of students, peasants, and laborers protested the takeover. They marched down the streets of China's big cities shouting, "Down with Japan! Down with power politics!" It seemed that a new spirit of national pride was awakening. But this spirit, deep though it was, could not save China. And, once again, the peasants suffered the most.

By this time, General Yuan had died and the whole country had been divided up among the former Manchu generals. These warlords, as they were called, began to fight among themselves, burning the villages and fields in their battles and tearing the country apart.

Sun Yat-sen and the weak Republic needed help to get control of China from the warlords. That aid came from an unexpected quarter—the new Communist government of Russia, now known as the Union of Soviet Socialist Republics.

There was a bond of kinship between the two countries because the peoples of both had suffered in the same way. Oppressed by their Czars, the Russian people had risen up in 1917, executed their rulers, and established a new kind of government. This government was based on the teachings of Karl Marx, a philosopher who lived in the late 1800s.

Marx believed that everything should belong to all the people. He advised revolution as the best way of overthrowing rulers, factory owners, and rich landlords. Then

26

the government, or state, would take control and the people would share equally in their country's goods. This form of government is known as Communism.

In establishing their Communist government, the Russians had developed methods that enabled them to defeat their enemies and become strong. Now they were ready to help the struggling Republic of China by giving them military training, advice, guns, and ammunition. Russia had good reason for wanting to see the new republic succeed. She had no allies in Europe, and a stronger China might prove a valuable friend in the future.

Although Dr. Sun wasn't interested in a Communist form of government, he accepted Russia's offer of help. Soon a Russian named Michael Borodin arrived in Canton to give advice. At the same time Dr. Sun began sending young officers to Moscow, Russia's capital, for training.

One of the officers to be sent was Chiang Kai-shek. Chiang was born in 1887, the only son of a wealthy landowner who lived in a small town near Shanghai. When Chiang was eight, his father died. Under Confucian law, this made him head of the household, though his mother managed the family affairs.

Chiang had a quick temper and a deep pride in his Chinese heritage. When he was seventeen, he quarreled with the corrupt Manchu officials in his town for over-taxing his family.

Chiang's mother, terrified that her son would be beheaded, quickly paid the sum. But Chiang was still furious, and shaved off his pigtail to show his hatred for the Manchus.

He decided on a military career and applied for entrance into the Chinese military academy, even though it was run by Manchu officers. There were only fourteen vacancies, and a thousand candidates were competing for them. The examination was difficult, but Chiang passed it and had to be accepted as a cadet.

During his two years at the academy, Chiang proved to be such a brilliant cadet that he qualified for specialized training in Japan. He was still there in 1911 when the revolutionaries rose in Hankow. He hurried back to join them so that he could do his share to rid the country of the hated Manchus.

In the World War I years, Chiang became a stockbroker in Shanghai, where he made a fortune. He also made many friends among the rich businessmen of the city. Then he joined Dr. Sun in Canton.

One day, Chiang saved Sun from assassination by the local Canton warlord. From then on, Dr. Sun trusted the young officer completely. When the new Whampoa Military Training School was established, Sun put Chiang Kai-shek in charge.

Chiang proved as brilliant a military instructor as he had been a cadet. By 1925, when Dr. Sun suddenly died, the young officer had a well-trained, well-disciplined army at his command. Since Chiang Kai-shek claimed he agreed with Dr. Sun's promise to help the poor peasants and workers, he seemed the logical man to head the government after Sun's death. As the Generalissimo of the Republic's new army, he was a man with a single purpose—to unite all China under his leadership.

4

The Long March

While Chiang Kai-shek was training the Nationalist army, another young man was working actively for the Communist cause in Hunan Province. His name was Mao Tse-tung. Mao was born in the little mountain village of Shao-shan near Changsha, capital of Hunan province. His parents had been poor peasants, but by hard work and thrift they had acquired about three acres of land, which they farmed with the help of hired men.

As the eldest son, Mao was expected to run the farm and keep the family accounts. So he was sent to the village school to learn how to read and write. His favorite books were historical novels about heroes who fought against China's corrupt dynasties. He liked to write poetry too.

Mao loved his gentle Buddhist mother, but he was often at odds with his stern Confucian father. He made his father angry by giving money to beggars during hard times. Worst of all, he showed no interest in the farm. Once he neglected the family fields to help some poor peasants get in their harvest ahead of the rain.

Mao wanted to return to school. At the age of 18, he entered a Western-style high school that had just opened in Changsha. Here, for the first time, Mao read about Dr. Sun Yat-sen and his revolutionaries. When the uprising took place in Hankow, he cut off his pigtail and persuaded ten other students to follow his example. Then he left school and joined the revolution, though the fighting was almost over by that time.

When the Republic was proclaimed, Mao went back to school and his books. He began reading Chinese translations of Western writers—the French philosopher Rousseau; Darwin, the English evolutionist; and Tolstoi, the Russian novelist.

Mao was a restless young man, and when he saw how badly the Republic was failing, he wanted to help his country. But he didn't know how to go about it. Perhaps, he thought, he might find his answer in Peking. In 1918, he went to the city and worked as an assistant librarian at Peking University.

There Mao found that many of the teachers had studied abroad and a large number of students were planning to go to universities in France or the United States. Small groups were holding classes on the writings of Karl Marx, on whose teachings Russian Communism had been founded.

Mao joined one of the groups. The more he studied about Marx, the more he became convinced that Communism was the answer to China's needs. He became a dedicated Communist and was among the twelve delegates who met secretly in Shanghai in 1921 to found the Chinese Communist Party.

From then on Mao went to cities to organize workers and encourage them to go on strike. He visited peasants in the countryside and urged them to rebel against their landlords. He was a magnetic speaker even though there was nothing imposing about his appearance. In contrast to General Chiang Kai-shek's military spruceness, Mao Tsetung's* clothes were

---

* During the Cultural Revolution, it was decided that Mao's given name— and his alone in the entire country—was to be spelled as one word.

Mao discusses Party ideology. The influence of Lenin and Marx is evident by their pictures on the wall.

sloppy. His socks drooped over his shoes. His sleeve cuffs were frayed and his trousers baggy.

But his appearance was deceiving. He was an athletic man who liked to swim and climb mountains and go on long hikes. Sometimes he took these hikes in the wintertime, wearing thin clothes, eating very little, and sleeping in the open without cover. Usually he was a man who loved food and comfort. But he explained to his friends that he was preparing himself for the years of struggle that he knew lay ahead before China could be unified under Communist rule.

In those early days, all the Communist parties around the world were under the supervision of an organization in Moscow called the Third International, or Comintern. The Comintern gave money and advice to people who wanted to start

Communist revolutions in their own countries. In return, it demanded complete obedience from its followers.

In 1925, shortly before Dr. Sun's death, the Comintern ordered the Chinese Communist Party to join with Dr. Sun's Nationalist forces. Only by working together could the two factions rid the country of warlords.

Along with other Communists, Mao went to Canton, where he was put in charge of Communist operations. Chiang Kai-shek's army would do the fighting. But the Communists would enlist the support of the peasants and workers.

Under Mao Tsetung, the Communists did their job well. They incited the peasants to rise against the landlords, and persuaded the city workers to damage machines, go on strike and start riots.

In the turmoil the Communists caused, Chiang Kai-shek's seasoned troops had no difficulty overthrowing the warlords. By the end of March, 1927, the Nationalist forces were in Shanghai. They controlled the country south of the Yangtze, with troops stationed at every conquered major city.

Chiang Kai-shek's victories had made him the most powerful man in China. He felt he no longer needed the help of the Communists, whom he had never trusted. He gave a gang of thugs, the Green Society, 5,000 rifles to kill all the Communists and their friends in Shanghai. And he sent out orders to Nationalist soldiers stationed in the cities he held to join in the slaughter.

The next day, without warning, the massacre began. Communist party officials and soldiers, workers in the city, and peasants in the country were cut down on the streets and in their fields or homes. The Russian adviser Borodin, fearing for his life, fled to Russia, taking Dr. Sun's widow with him.

Only Mao and a few Communists managed to escape. They

went into hiding until they received new orders from the Comintern in Russia. The Chinese Communist Party was to raise an army of workers and peasants to overthrow the Nationalists. This was the beginning of Civil War in China.

Mao gathered an army of peasants in his home province of Hunan, and led them against Changsha, its capital city. But the untrained peasant army was no match for the Nationalist troops. Moreover, the workers inside the city were so afraid of another massacre that they refused to join in the uprising. Mao's peasant recruits were easily overpowered and slaughtered. He himself was captured. Fortunately, his captors didn't know who he was, and he was able to bribe his way to freedom.

Rejoining the remnants of his army, Mao led them into the desolate wilderness of the nearby Chingkangshan mountains. As the months went by, units from other Communist armies began trickling into Mao's hideout. They all told the same story. The Comintern's order had ended in disaster. Everywhere the uprisings had met with defeat.

Slowly but steadily, the Communist forces on Chingkangshan grew, and Chiang Kai-shek became worried. He sent a number of expeditions to flush them out. But all expeditions failed because of the loyalty of the peasants who lived nearby.

The peasants warned Mao when Nationalist troops approached. They stole ammunition and guns from the soldiers and gave them to the Communists. And they led the Nationalists into ambushes, where the Communists could cut them down easily. These methods of guerrilla warfare, which Mao Tsetung taught the peasants, had all been described in the historical novels of ancient China which he had read as a boy. Now he was putting them to good use. He formulated them into a set of rules for his men to follow. "If the enemy advances, we retreat. If the enemy halts and encamps, we harass. If the enemy seeks to avoid battle, we attack. If the enemy retreats, we pursue."

While the Communists were in Chingkangshan, they reorganized their battered army. They called it the Red Army because red had been chosen by the Russians as the official Communist color. But red also has a special meaning in China, where for centuries it has been the color of joy and celebration. Young brides wore red instead of white. Babies were dressed in red. And at festivals children put on gay red clothes. So people were drawn to the very name of the Red Army.

Nevertheless, it was going to be hard to change their opinion about soldiers in general. For centuries, army men had been hated by the Chinese because of their arrogant behavior. But the Red Army was very different from other armies in China. They wanted soldiers who were dedicated to serving the people. They would be ready to help the peasants in their fields and take their side against the landlords who oppressed them. By convincing the peasants that the Red Army had their interests at heart, a strong bond would be built up between them. And the peasants could be counted on to help the Communist soldiers everywhere, just as they had helped them at Chingkangshan.

One of the first things Red Army officers did was to lay down strict rules of conduct for the soldiers. These rules were based on common courtesy, something no Chinese soldier ever before had practiced. "Don't take anything from workers or peasants. Speak politely. Pay fairly for whatever you buy. Return everything you borrow. Pay for anything you damage. These rules, which were strictly enforced, made the Red

Army welcome almost everywhere it went.

In August of 1933, Chiang Kai-shek made an all-out effort to flush the Communists from their mountain retreat. He gathered together a million men and four hundred airplanes. He removed the peasants and put them behind his lines so that they were no longer able to help the Communists. And he built fortresses at intervals all around the mountains, creating such a tight blockade that no food could get through.

The Red Army leaders realized they would have to leave the mountain camp and find a new refuge. Their only safety lay in reaching a small Communist settlement in remote Shensi province, 6,000 miles to the northwest. So the Red Army forced its way through the blockade and set out on the long trek westward.

There were some 100,000 soldiers in the army. But many of them were accompanied by wives and children, swelling the number to 200,000. This great body of people set off across south China. All along the way, they fought off Nationalist forces. Nationalist planes flew overhead, dropping bombs and killing or wounding many Communists.

Mao Tsetung's second wife, Ho Tzu-chen, was hit by shrapnel and had to be carried on a stretcher. His first wife had been executed by the Nationalists in 1930. It was common for many Communist women to fight with the men. The army not only had women commanders but also a whole regiment of 2,000 women.

Children of eleven and twelve did their share too. These Young Vanguards served as messengers and orderlies. But the women who could not fight and the younger children were left in friendly villages along the way.

By the time the Red Army reached the Yangtze, 25,000 soldiers were either killed or wounded. Leaving the wounded with friendly peasants, the army pressed on—only to find the Yangtze guarded by Nationalist forces. But they managed to slip by the guards, taking several boats from the enemy's camp to ferry themselves across the rushing river.

Now they entered the wilderness of the Great Snowy Mountains, the Tah-sueh Shan, inhabited only by wild Yi tribes. For centuries, the Yi, who hated the Chinese, had raided the lowlands, kidnapping peasants and making them their slaves. The Nationalists were sure the Yi would destroy the Red Army. But the courtesy of the Communist soldiers won the tribesmen over. Instead of making war, they signed a friendship pact and helped them.

The way led over towering snowclad mountains and across stormy rivers. The soldiers were not dressed for such climate and terrain. They wore only thin clothing and cloth sandals, and many of them froze to death.

Things were no better when the Red Army reached the warm lowlands of Szechuan Province. This region was patrolled by Nationalist units, and the Red Army fought many skirmishes with them. Again they were helped by loyal peasants, who hid and fed the soldiers and acted as lookouts and guides.

To escape the Nationalists, the Communists made their way westward to the desolate and treacherous bogs of the Tibetan Grasslands. The bogs were a sea of thick mud, overgrown by grass clumps, that stretched away for miles. The soldiers had to jump from clump to clump, and those who made a single misstep were swallowed in the mud.

Beyond the bogs, the Red Army came to more desolate wastelands inhabited by wild Tibetan tribesmen who refused all offers of friendship. They hid their food from the starving soldiers, and shot at them from behind rocks with guns the Nationalists had given them. They also rolled huge boulders down on the soldiers as they filed through narrow ravines.

Finally, toward the end of October, 1935, a pitiful remnant of the Red Army reached the little settlement of Shensi Province. There were only 7,000 survivors from Chingkanshan, although other recruits had joined along the way, bringing the number to 20,000. Their journey had lasted 386 days and came to be known as the Long March. No other army in history had ever made so long a march under such terrible conditions.

The province of Shensi was one of the poorest and most desolate in China. Mountains, plains, hills, ravines—all were covered by a layer of fine silt called loess. In some places, the loess was five hundred feet deep. There was little rainfall most of the year. But in the summer season, sudden downpours would sometimes turn the earth into flowing rivers of mud, which washed away the terraced fields. This made farming of the loess very perilous. In all China, the area was always the hardest hit by famine.

The Communists had already set up their own government here. They forced the landlords to lower rents. And they helped the peasants start new farms and showed them ways to increase their crop yield. For the first time in centuries, a part of the loess country was prospering.

Mao Tsetung established his base at Yenan, the capital of Shensi Province. Like the homes of the peasants around him, his house was a cave dug into the soft loess cliffs.

By this time, Mao had emerged as the leader of the Chinese Communist Party. He had won the loyalty of the soldiers by his concern for their suffering on the Long March. His unfailing good spirits had kept their courage up. And his determination to win earned him their trust. Now they were ready to follow him anywhere.

In the past months, Mao had realized two things. One was that the peasants, who were far more numerous than the workers, would have to be the backbone of any successful revolution in China. The other was that guerrilla warfare was the only means by which the weak Red Army could fight the strong Nationalist forces.

The Russian Communists had exactly opposite theories about how revolution should be waged. They claimed that only workers could be used, and that guerrilla warfare could never take the place of great popular uprisings. They were angry with Mao Tsetung for not following their advice. He was too independent for them. Though they had wanted an ally in China, they didn't want one who challenged their authority when he chose. From then on, Russia gave the Chinese Communists no more money, supplies or advice.

Without any friends, it did not look as if the little Chinese Communist settlement would last for long. Chiang Kai-shek still sent Nationalist planes over Yenan on frequent bombing raids, there were numerous ground battles. The Communists were constantly on the run.

By this time, the Nationalist government was well established in China. It was a government that catered to the business people and rich landlords. But the peasants and workers were no better off than before.

Chiang Kai-shek ignored his promise to carry out Dr. Sun Yat-sen's dream of a democracy. His government was a dictatorship in which the people had no voice. Taxes were still high and officials were still corrupt. The landlords were still charging the peasants high rental fees and turning them off the land when they could not pay. Workers were still receiving only a few cents a day. When they formed labor unions and tried to strike for higher wages, their employers simply called in the Nationalist soldiers, who gunned them down.

Nothing had changed for women either. Though the Nationalist government had promised equal education and banned slavery and foot binding, the laws were never enforced.

The peasants continued to suffer from floods, droughts, and famines. One of the worst of these famines hit the Northwest region of China in 1929 and lasted three years. Millions of peasants died, while the businessmen and landlords in the region horded wheat, which they planned to sell at high prices.

Even though conditions were so terrible, few peasants or workers dared criticize the government. Chiang Kai-shek's Secret Police were everywhere, arresting and executing those who spoke out against the Nationalists.

To make matters worse, in 1931 Japanese troops invaded Manchuria, and two years later occupied North China.

In the summer of 1937, they took Peking; in the fall, Shanghai fell to them. Then the Japanese forces marched up the Yangtze Valley and took Nanking, Chiang Kai-shek's capital.

Chiang Kai-shek, his government, and most of his army had already retreated upriver to Hankow. From there, they were pushed up the Yangtze to Chungking. There the Generalissimo set up his wartime capital. Thereafter, he and his army did little fighting. He felt there was no chance of winning against the strong Japanese forces.

But the Communists were active. They made lightning strikes on small enemy patrols. And they taught the peasants how to lay mines and where to hide themselves and their food supplies whenever Japanese soldiers approached their villages.

By using guerrilla tactics, the Communists terrified the Japanese. And, as a result, the Communists took control of whole areas, forcing the Japanese out.

The Communists governed these liberated areas so fairly that they won the loyalty and love of the peasants.

Meanwhile World War II had broken out in Europe, and Japan allied herself with Germany. In 1941, the Japanese bombed Pearl Harbor and the United States entered the war. Chiang Kai-shek allied his government with the United States in the hope the Americans would help him against the Japanese and the Communists.

President Franklin D. Roosevelt sent General Joseph Stilwell to work with the Generalissimo. Stilwell found a corrupt government in Chungking. Nationalist generals were secretly trading with the Japanese, and government officials were heavily taxing the people and pocketing the money. Everywhere there was illness, filth, and starvation.

Chiang Kai-shek demanded $500,000,000 from the United States to help him carry on the war. But when he received the money, it too, ended in the bank accounts of government officials. Even Chiang's soldiers were poorly fed and clothed, and they were mistreated by their officers. He refused to use the guns and ammunition he received from the United States against the Japanese. Instead, he planned to save them to fight the Communists when the war with Japan was over.

Japan surrendered in 1945. And in China, once again the country hovered on the brink of Civil War. President Truman sent General George C. Marshall to make peace between Chiang Kai-shek and Mao Tsetung. But he failed, and in 1947 fighting began again.

The United States sent large military supplies to back her old ally Chiang Kai-shek. With these supplies his Nationalist army was far stronger than the Red Army. But the Communist soldiers used their guerrilla tactics again. They roamed the countryside of north China, fighting weak Nationalist patrols and recruiting soldiers from among the many peasants they had trained during the war with Japan.

Finally the Red Army, or People's Liberation Army (PLA), became strong enough to attack the main Nationalist forces which were holding the cities. Beginning in Manchuria, the PLA marched south. All along the way, thousands of Nationalist soldiers deserted to them, bringing along their guns, amunition, and even American tanks. City after city fell.

In January of 1949, the Communists were at the gates of Peking. The Nationalist garrison which held the city fled to the southern banks of the Yangtze River.

In May the Communists reached the Yangtze. No one believed they could cross those turbulent waters, protected by heavy Nationalist guns which lined the southern banks. But the peasants in the vicinity again came to the aid of the Communist soldiers. They secretly gathered together thousands of small boats and hid them in the marshes along the northern banks of the river.

One dark night, with the peasants acting as steersmen, the Red Army started across the river in the flimsy boats. The Nationalists opened fire, capsizing many boats. The soldiers and peasants in them were either drowned or killed.

But others kept on coming. Soon they were swarming up the southern bank of the river. The Nationalist forces broke and fled. Nanking, their capital city, fell. The Communists continued to pursue them as they retreated southward. But in midsummer of 1949, protected by battleships of the United States Navy, the Nationalists, led by Chiang Kai-shek, managed to escape to the island of Taiwan.

On October 1, 1949, Mao Tsetung stood on the rostrum atop the gate of Tien An Men (Gate of Heavenly Peace) in Peking, which the Communists had chosen for their new capital. Before him passed a great parade of victorious Red soldiers, both men and women, wearing their green uniforms with red stars on their caps.

Regiments of blue-coated peasants, who had helped the Red Soldiers all along the way, marched proudly beside them waving red flags. And there were thousands of children, who had acted as lookouts and scouts.

Millions of people packed the square. When Mao Tsetung solemnly announced the founding of the People's Republic of China, they all cheered. They were sure that at last, after so much suffering, a new and better life awaited them. Mao Tsetung had promised it.

5

The People's Republic of China Sets Its Course

Mao's victorious speech from the rostrum couldn't hide the fact that China was a shambles. Twelve years of war had destroyed or damaged most of the factories. Roads, railways, and bridges were ruined.

The new government immediately went into action. It took over all food supplies and sold them at fixed low prices. Then, to make sure that everyone got an equal share, it distributed ration cards. No one could buy food without a ration card. At the same time, the government closed all the private banks and set up its own State Bank. This was done to keep tight control of money. The Red Army repaired railways, roads, and bridges. City people were organized to clean up the slums. Everyone worked—even the beggars, who were no longer allowed to live by begging.

The narrow, garbage-heaped lanes of Shanghai's slum districts were among the worst in the world. Thousands of men, women, and children, with brooms, shovels, baskets, and wheelbarrows, started to clean up the filth.

Bit by bit, as the days and months went by, they cleared the lanes and widened them. They fixed some of the tottering old houses, and tore down the worst of them. Some of the hovels were only straw mats patched together and raised in the middle so that a whole family could crawl under for shelter. Using only hand tools, the workers then built small apartment buildings in the cleared spaces. It would take many years to clean up a city as dirty and as huge as Shanghai, but a beginning had at last been made.

Gradually, the factories in the cities were also repaired and put back into use. Under the Nationalists, they had belonged to private businessmen. Now the State took the factories over, and hired the owners to run them. They were paid a percentage of the profits as their wages. However as soon as managers representing the State could be trained, the owners were to be retired on pensions.

One of the worst problems the Chinese Communists had to face was opium addiction. Millions of people in all parts of China were still smoking opium. The Communists tackled the problem in several ways. They taught young people that they were important to their government. They made them realize that they could not serve the State if they were addicted to the drug. The young people were inspired by the new spirit in China, and so it wasn't hard to persuade them not to take up the habit.

To help the addicts, the Communists organized anti-opium committees to treat them at home, in clinics, or in hospitals.

Then they concentrated on the peasants who were raising opium poppies, instead of rice or wheat, because opium brought more money. Once the peasants realized they could no longer sell their opium, since the government had prohibited it, and that food brought them the highest prices, they went back to growing rice, wheat, and millet.

There was only one other source from which opium could come—through smugglers. The Communists sought out the smugglers and sent them to labor camps, where they were given lessons in Communism until their thinking had changed. The campaign worked, and by 1953 China's drug problem was almost eliminated.

Another campaign which the Communists launched was to promote equal rights for women. All through the Civil War, the Communists had promised women they would get a fair deal in the new government. Mao himself had a deep admiration for their bravery. He claimed that on the Long March women had proved far more courageous than the men.

To help the women take advantage of their new rights,

the State sent *kan-pu,* or representatives, to every village and remote community. The *kan-pu* ordered an end to the selling of children. They saw that all concubines and slaves were released and given work to make them independent. They informed unhappily married women, especially young girls who had been sold as brides to much older men, that they had a right to divorce. And they rigidly enforced the ban against foot binding.

At the same time, the *kan-pu* instructed both men and women on the new order of things. It was especially hard for the men to accept the fact that women had an equal right to go to school, have a career, and do as they pleased instead of blindly obeying their husbands. It was just as hard for many women to take advantage of this new-found freedom.

The *kan-pu* had other duties in the countryside too. A few months after the founding of the People's Republic of China, the State launched a Land Reform program. The goal was to take all the land from the rich landlords and divide it among the peasants. But the government wanted the peasants in each village to do the job themselves. By so doing, they would realize that they no longer needed to fear the landlords.

The *kan-pu* encouraged the peasants to hold "speak bitter" meetings. At the meetings the peasants accused the terrified landlords, who had to sit and listen:

"You took my land, and we had to become beggars."

"You took my son from me and let him die."

"You took so much of my harvest every year that there wasn't enough for us to eat. And I had to sell two of my children."

"You paid me hardly anything for working your land."

"You cheated me by making me pay such high rents

that two of my children starved to death."

Finally the peasants demanded that the landlords give up their land. The landlords were afraid to object, and the land was redistributed by the *kan-pu*.

Those landowners who had not been too harsh received some land, which they had to work themselves. But the landlords who had been cruel or who had helped the Nationalists and the Japanese were tried by People's Courts. Many were sentenced to labor camps. Many more were sentenced to death. Tens of thousands of landlords were publicly executed before the government stepped in and put an end to the killing.

By 1952, the Land Reform movement came to an end. All over China, millions of poor peasants held land for the first time in their lives.

But the Communists knew that this wouldn't solve the food problem. Farming small plots of land individually isn't effiicient. The peasants would have to learn to work together. So, the year after Land Reform, the *kan-pu* suggested that the peasants form "mutual aid" teams. Each team, which was made up of ten families, would keep its own plots of land as well as share animals, farm tools, and labor.

The peasants discovered that cooperation paid off in better crops. The next step was to join eight or nine mutual aid teams together into a cooperative. Under this system the peasants worked the land together. Then the money from the crops was divided among the members of the cooperative according to the amount of land they owned and the number of hours they worked. This resulted in another increase of crops.

However, it was much harder to persuade the peasants to take the next step. That was to turn their cooperatives into

A commune brings in the harvest near
the Red Flag Canal which they built.

collective farms in which all the land would be owned jointly
by the peasants. Individual farmers would be paid only for
their work, which was to be measured by work points.

Many peasants protested. So the government allowed each
one to keep a small plot of his own where he could grow
vegetables. He was also allowed to have a few farm animals—
pigs, hens, and sheep. The peasants accepted this plan,
though they were not very pleased about it.

By 1957 all of China's farmland had been divided into
collectives. Now the final step was taken. Six or more
collectives were united into a single commune. Today there
are about 75,000 communes in China. Each one is made
up of 15,000 families. With so many people in a commune,
it is possible to raise a work force large enough to build
such projects as dams, irrigation canals, and reservoirs to
benefit the whole area. The communes also provide hospitals,
schools, and "homes of respect" for those elderly persons

who have no relatives to care for them. The money for these services is provided by the work teams and the brigades, which pay small amounts into the communal fund.

The communes are self-governing on the local level. This self-governing begins with the lowest unit, the work team. Each work team elects several representatives, who meet regularly to handle the business of the team. They assign the work, sell the produce, pay the taxes, and then divide the rest of the money among the peasants of their unit according to work points. They also settle disputes.

Representatives from the work team are chosen to sit on the Brigade Council, which coordinates the efforts of the various work teams. The Brigade Council chooses members to represent it at the Commune Congress. And the Commune Congress sends representatives to the County Congress. Representatives of the County Congress go to the large Provincial Congress. Each of these congresses coordinates the work of those below it.

Finally, the large Provincial Congress elects representatives to sit on the National People's Congress, which gathers only once a year in Peking. Sometimes even this yearly meeting doesn't take place. But whenever it does, the Congress elects a Standing Committee from among its members. This committee represents the National People's Congress in the capital and stays in office until the next election is held.

The Chairman of the Standing Committee becomes the President of the country. When the 1,141 members of the first Congress met in September, 1954, they elected Mao Tsetung as the President.

The President, however, holds no real power. All the power

in China is held by the Central Committee of the Chinese Communist Party. Only 2 per cent of the people belong to the Party. You can't just decide to join it. You have to be sponsored by two Party members and then send in a written application and take an examination on the principles of Communism. Your daily life is watched to see if you are living up to those principles by helping the people in your community and taking an active part in political study groups. Finally, if you are accepted, you must take an oath to dedicate all your spare time to working for the Party in whatever task it gives you.

You have to belong to the party even to serve as a *kan-pu* in the communes. And only Party members can belong to the Central Committee. The full Central Committee has 170 members. It does the routine work of the Party. But the most powerful unit of government is a small group elected from the Central Committee. This group, which today contains twenty-one members, is the Politburo. The Politburo itself has a Standing Committee of nine members. It is these nine members who actually decide the policies China will follow. The Chairman of the Politburo is the most powerful man in all China. For years that post has been held by Chairman Mao Tsetung.

Once the policies have been decided, they are presented to the National People's Congress. The Congress cannot reject the policies that come from the Politburo. It simply puts its stamp of approval on them and then hands the policies down to the *kan-pu* who are stationed in every commune. Each commune is given a crop quota to fullfill, and it is told what construction jobs to work on. The congresses and the councils then decide upon the best ways of carrying out the government directives.

If the peasants feel that the policies are unreasonable, they can object. The *kan-pu*, who also acts as the "Party's eyes and ears among the masses," will report these complaints. Then adjustments are made until everyone is satisfied. In this way, the Communists hope to prevent uprisings.

The *kan-pu* and the congresses usually work well together, because the members of the congresses and councils have all been chosen from names submitted to the people by the *kan-pu*.

To the Chinese, who for centuries have known only the will of emperors and dictators, this kind of government is a step toward self-rule.

 **6**

The Great Leap and the Cultural Revolution

Every five years, the Politburo establishes new goals for the country. They are called Five-Year Plans, and the first one began in 1952. It set high quotas for food production, heavy industry, and mining.

The newspapers, which were government-owned, prepared the people for the great drive by appealing to their patriotism. The people responded by working hard. At the end of five years, food production had doubled. New industries had opened. China had built her first trucks, her first oil tanker, and her first light airplanes.

But though the country had made great advances, she was still far behind the industrialized world. Mao Tsetung was convinced that, with a great deal more effort, China could catch up in the next five years. He called the second Five-Year Plan the Great Leap Forward.

One of the biggest goals of the Great Leap Forward was for the increased output of steel. But China had very few modern rolling mills to produce steel, though big steel plants were in the works. The Soviet Union had sent dozens of technicians to guide Chinese engineers in building them.

Meanwhile, the government asked the people to produce steel by hand. Tens of thousands of peasants were urged to build cement furnaces in their backyards. Digging out coal and iron ore from small deposits in their vicinity, they did

Workers take the place of trucks and cranes.

the smelting when work in the fields was over.

Everything seemed to be going well during the first year of the Great Leap. Then the Soviet and Chinese governments quarreled. China felt that the Soviet Union was slipping away from true Communism by giving people bonuses for extra work instead of considering it their patriotic duty to do the work. The Chinese called it "revisionism." The Soviet Union, who felt she was the leader of the Communist world, resented China's criticisms.

The quarrel became so bitter that the U.S.S.R. recalled her technicians. They left China, taking their plans with them. All work on the factories came to a halt until Chinese engineers could finish the job.

As for the millions of tons of steel the peasants had produced it turned out to be of very poor quality. The steel could be used only to make small farm implements, such as hoes, spades, and ploughshares.

Farming also was not going well. For three years in a row, heavy floods, droughts, and insect pests ruined many crops. To make matters worse, domineering *kan-pu* who knew nothing about agriculture had been interfering with the farming. They made peasants plant seeds so deep that they rotted in the ground. And they took millions of people away from the fields during the critical growing period to work on dams and irrigation systems.

The Central Committee knew nothing of what was going on because the *kan-pu* falsified all their reports to make them surpass the quotas that had been set. For the first time since the People's Republic was founded, China came close to serious famine. Anger and unrest flared across the country, and there were even some uprisings.

The government in Peking acted quickly. The domineering *kan-pu* were replaced, and the peasants were given back full control of their farming. Chairman Mao publicly admitted his mistake in launching the Great Leap Foward. He resigned the post of President, and Liu Shao-chi, one of his companions on the Long March, took his place. It was announced that Liu would succeed to the powerful Chairmanship of the Politburo when Mao died.

During the third Five-Year Plan, Chinese engineers completed the iron and steel mills. Once more, all industry surged ahead. Then, in 1964, China astonished the world by exploding her first atomic bomb in the deserts of Sinkiang province.

The Chinese were proud because prosperity had returned to their land. And though they knew their country still had far to go to catch up to the other big nations, it seemed to them that she was well on the way.

Despite all these successes, Chairman Mao was becoming increasingly worried. He felt that the old spirit of loyalty and service that the Chinese Communist Party had shown throughout the revolution was dying out. Disturbing reports were coming to him of *kan-pu* in remote districts who were cutting down on the work points of the peasants so they could take the extra money themselves. Some of the *kan-pu* were even joining with former landlords to force the peasants to pay rent for their land.

The children of workers and peasants were not being enrolled in the big universities. Instead, most of the student bodies were made up of the children of intellectuals and former businessmen, who were still wealthy from the pensions they received.

Worst of all, the country was splitting into two factions or groups—the Mao faction and the faction that was behind Liu Shao-chi. Liu Shao-chi and his faction wanted to patch things up with the Soviet Union and follow their way of doing things. To Mao that meant gradually slipping back into the old days. He decided that China needed a revolution to wake the people up. He chose the students to lead it because they would be the future rulers of China. And he wanted them to understand what revolution was all about.

The students were formed into a new organization called the Red Guards in honor of the Red Army of the civil war. Formal schooling was dropped, and the students began to study the meaning of revolution. Their textbook was a little red book entitled *The Thoughts of Chairman Mao.* It contained many of Mao's sayings, which were full of practical advice on how to be a good Communist.

In August of 1966, the study period came to an end. All schools and colleges were closed, and the Great Proletarian Cultural Revolution began. Carrying their little red books, millions of students set out across the country.

Everywhere they went, the Red Guards held study classes to discuss the sayings of Mao Tsetung. Soon almost everyone in China had a little red book and was quoting Mao and attending study classes. Everyone vowed to exert himself to the utmost to please Chairman Mao, "Our Red Sun."

At first the Revolution went smoothly. But as time went by, it began to change. The Red Guards became more and more arrogant. They accused honored, long-time Party officials of revisionism and paraded them around the streets in dunce caps. They defaced ancient temples, which had been turned into museums, and smashed some of the priceless

Carrying their little red books, millions of
Red Guards set out across the country.

objects in them because they represented the old things of
China.

Soon the Red Guards and Liu Shao-chi factions were
battling one another. Workers in the city and peasants in
some parts of the country joined one side or the other. Fighting broke out everywhere.

No one really knows how many people were killed during
the Cultural Revolution. But the turmoil was so great that
China was once again threatened by civil war. To save the
country, the Cultural Revolution was brought to an abrupt

end in the spring of 1967, less than a year after it had been started. By this time Mao Tsetung's group had proved triumphant. Liu Shao-chi was ousted from the presidency, and he disappeared from sight.

The millions of Red Guards were either sent back to their homes or shipped off to remote areas to work with the peasants and learn from them. Some of the students went willingly. Others, angered at having their education cut off so abruptly, continued to fight. It took two years before the Red Army could quiet the unrest.

The commander of the army was Lin Piao, Minister of Defense in the powerful Politburo. Nicknamed Tiger Cat Lin, he was a brilliant militarist and propagandist. Lin Piao became a hero. The newspapers referred to him as "Chairman Mao's close comrade in arms."

In 1969, Lin was named Deputy Chairman and Mao's successor in place of Liu Shao-chi. By 1970 the Defense Minister had become so prominent that people were wearing badges showing the profiles of both Chairman Mao and Deputy Chairman Lin.

But in the summer of 1971, Lin suddenly disappeared. On August 1, the anniversary of the founding of the People's Liberation Army, he wasn't even mentioned in speeches. Instead, a government radio broadcaster quoted one of Chairman Mao's sayings, "The Party commands the gun, and the gun must never be allowed to command the Party."

"The army must place itself under the party's absolute leadership." In the days that followed, that phrase was repeated again and again, both on broadcasts and in the government-controlled newspapers.

There were rumors that Lin was trying to betray Chairman Mao and put the army in command of the country. Then, in September, there was a news story of a plane crash on the Mongolian frontier. Many people thought that it had carried Lin Piao to his death. But not until the summer of 1972 was the story given to the world.

Lin Piao and several top army officials had been plotting to assassinate Chairman Mao and take over the People's Republic of China. When the plot was discovered, Lin Piao tried to escape to the Soviet Union with his wife and seven other army officials in an army plane. The plane crashed at the border, and everyone aboard was killed.

By now, the Cultural Revolution was over and the country was back to normal. The little red books of Chairman Mao's thoughts were still widely read and studied, although there were not so many slogans. The large Mao buttons that had been worn during the revolution began to disappear along with many of the huge public statues of the Chairman. People seemed much more relaxed.

There were many other changes. One new rule stated that everyone, no matter what his official position or profession, had to spend two or three months a year working either in a factory or in a commune. Mao Tsetung hoped that, by bringing professional people closer together with workers and peasants, he would keep a modern scholar class from developing. If the intelligensia, as such a class is known today, should gain control over the People's Republic, it might again govern China to satisfy its own interests.

Another rule was that high school graduates could no longer go directly to college. They would have to spend two or three years working either in a factory or in a commune. At the end of that time, the factory workers or the people in the commune would decide whether these young people showed enough of the right political spirit to go on to college. And the professors would then judge their academic abilities.

7

Foreign Affairs

At the time of its founding, the People's Republic of China had few allies. Even the Soviet leaders continued to treat her coldly, for they still distrusted Mao Tsetung.

He received a cool welcome when he visited Moscow following the founding of the new republic. And he had difficulty getting any concessions from the Russians. They did agree reluctantly to give back some of the territory in Manchuria that they had taken from the Japanese during World War II. They also promised to return some of the machinery they had stripped from Manchurian factories.

The Russians did sign trade agreements with China and made pacts of friendship. But they offered no free aid. Instead they lent money to the Chinese at high interest rates.

Mao Tsetung had to accept their terms. China was a poor nation and needed help to strengthen herself. She certainly couldn't afford any more war. Yet, in 1950, she found herself fighting in Korea which borders China on the northeast.

After World War II, the United Nations had guided the division of Korea into two sections — North Korea, which was Communist, and South Korea, which called itself a democracy. Then, in 1950, the North Korean army marched into South Korea and took the capital city of Seoul. The United Nations troops, which were made up primarily of American forces, drove back the North Koreans.

The People's Republic of China watched as General Douglas MacArthur and his UN troops marched up the Korean peninsula closer and closer to the Yalu River, which forms the boundary between China and Korea. Several times, China warned MacArthur that if he came too close the Chinese would come to the aid of the North Koreans.

General MacArthur ignored the warning. Then suddenly, as he neared the Yalu, his forces were met by a huge Chinese army. It called itself the People's Volunteer Army, but it was really made up of crack divisions from the Red Army. During the next three years, both sides lost many men. One of them was Mao Tsetung's own son. Finally, in 1953, a truce was declared.

Although the Korean War was over, China felt she still had to keep up her guard. The United States still recognized Chiang Kai-shek as the rightful leader of the Chinese, and throughout the 1950s the American government gave economic and military aid to him. Ships from the U.S. fleet constantly patrolled the Formosa Straits between the Chinese mainland and Taiwan to protect it from any attempt at invasion by the Communists.

But it was Chiang Kai-shek himself who talked year after year about invading the mainland. He actually invaded the two small islands of Quemoy and Matsu, which lay some twenty-five miles off the south China coast.

The People's Republic of China was afraid that one day, with the backing of the United States, the Nationalist forces would attempt a major invasion of the mainland. So great was their concern that they built a railroad line through the rocky mountains that line the coast facing Taiwan. Over this railroad they transported troops and weapons and fortified the shore with heavy guns.

At the same time that Taiwan was causing the Chinese Communists so much concern, trouble broke out in Tibet. Through the centuries, Tibet had been sometimes independent and sometimes a part of China. She had slipped from Chinese control during the last years of the Ching Dynasty. But in 1950 the People's Republic of China had taken her over again. However, a pact signed with the Dalai Lama, the political and spiritual leader of Tibet, allowed him to keep his power and his own form of government.

Then in the mid-1950s, the fierce Tibetan tribesmen rebelled, and the revolt spread across the country. It was rumored that agents of the United States had instigated the revolt. The Red Army sent several crack divisions to put it down. The uprising was finally quelled, and the Dalai Lama fled to India.

Almost as soon as the Tibetan situation was settled, China found herself at odds over the boundary between India and Tibet. China claimed that the border line that the British had drawn up, after their invasion of Tibet in the 1800s, had robbed Tibet of 32,000 square miles of territory.

For several months, there were skirmishes between

Chinese and Indian troops along the border. Finally the Chinese took over part of it — a desolate plateau too cold and barren for any use except one, the one for which the Chinese wanted it.

They began to build a railway through it — a railway that today stretches clear across Tibet to the oil-rich province of Sinkiang, in far northwest China. Over this railway the Chinese would be able to transport troops, weapons, and fuel in case of an invasion from India. China's fear was well grounded, for the Dalai Lama was rousing the sympathy of Western nations with his fervent pleas to free his homeland.

Then the threat of war and invasion moved from Taiwan and India to Southeast Asia, where the United States had plunged herself into the troubled affairs of Vietnam.

In 1954 Vietnam had been divided into two countries, Communist North Vietnam and democratic South Vietnam. But the government of South Vietnam was unpopular with many peasants, who joined the Vietcong, a secret Communist organization. When the Vietcong grew strong enough, they staged an uprising to take over all South Vietnam. The Vietcong were helped by North Vietnam, which in turn was aided by China and the Soviet Union. South Vietnam was helped by the United States and her allies.

Hundreds of thousands of American troops were sent to fight beside the South Vietnamese soldiers. American planes flew on bombing missions over North Vietnam. Several strayed across the border into China and were shot down. China vowed to enter the war on the side of the North Vietnamese if it was invaded.

The Chinese Communists voiced their hatred of America

everywhere. School children sang songs about making war on Yankee imperialists. There were marches and demonstrations. By this time, the gap between China and the United States had grown so wide that it looked as though it could never be closed.

On the other hand, China's relations with most other nations had been improving over the years. By the beginning of the Cultural Revolution, she had exchanged ambassadors with forty-one countries, including England and France. Then, while the Cultural Revolution was in progress, she broke off all these ties and isolated herself from the world — except for the Soviet Union.

The ill-feeling between China and the Soviet Union had been growing rapidly worse ever since 1960, when the Soviet Union had withdrawn her technicians from China. During the Cultural Revolution, the two countries had a bitter argument over the border line between Soviet Siberia and China's Northeast region.

In the days of the Czars the Russians had forced the weak Ching Emperor to give them part of what was then called Manchuria. There they were able to build the port of Vladivostok on the Pacific Ocean. Now China was asking the Russians to admit that the Czars had taken the land wrongfully. If the Russians would do so, China promised to stop insisting on its return.

But the Soviet Union refused to admit anything, and border clashes flared out. The fighting spread, and soon Chinese and Soviet patrols were attacking each other along a 4,500-mile frontier. Part of this frontier lies between Inner Mongolia, which China governs, and the People's Republic of Outer Mongolia. Outer Mongolia rules itself, but it has strong ties with the Soviet Union. So it permitted the U.S.S.R. to station a million and a half troops along its border to face the long line of Chinese troops to the south.

The Soviet Union built barracks and airfields in Outer Mongolia and installed rockets with nuclear warheads. Then long-range bombers arrived and began to practice maneuvers.

Was the Soviet Union preparing to launch a war to wipe out China's small store of atomic weapons and materials? They were stockpiled within easy reach in western Kansu, which is on the northern border of Inner Mongolia. Chairman Mao and the Politburo took action at once.

The atomic material was transferred to Tibet and hidden in rugged mountainous areas. The Chinese people were urged to begin digging air-raid shelters. Soon almost every village and town in China had its own underground shelter where food supplies were stored. The foundations of cities were honeycombed with tunnels which were re-enforced with concrete arches and brick walls. First-aid stations and food depots were set up at intervals.

By the fall of 1969, tensions had begun to relax. Soviet Premier Aleksei Kosygin went to Peking to negotiate on the disputed boundaries. But so far nothing has been settled. There are still some border clashes, and the fear of a Russian attack is still strong in China. Perhaps it was because of this fear that after the Cultural Revolution, China hurried to establish old diplomatic relations and make new ties.

One of these new ties was with the United States. Richard M. Nixon, President of the United States, seemed the least likely of men to move toward closing the gap between his country and the People's Republic of China. Ever since he had been a Senator and, later, Vice President, he had been strongly opposed to recognizing the Communist government in Peking or giving it a seat in the United Nations.

But as his first term in office drew to a close, President Nixon changed his views. In 1971, he sent his personal adviser, Dr. Henry Kissinger, to Peking to arrange a visit there for him. That visit took place in February of the following year. President Nixon met with Chairman Mao Tsetung and spent many hours in conference with Premier Chou En-lai, the Minister of Foreign Affairs.

Premier Chou, seventy-five years old, is considered one of the most able diplomats in the world. His parents belonged to the wealthy scholar class, but young Chou was a Communist from his student days. He studied in Japan and in France, and later helped to organize Chinese Communist groups in Paris and Berlin.

Chou was back in China leading labor revolts in Shanghai when Chiang Kai-shek ordered the massacre of Communists. He escaped and joined the Red Army on the Long March. Since then, he has served as an adviser in foreign affairs and a trouble shooter at home.

At the close of their lengthy meetings, Premier Chou and

Left to right: Chou En-lai, the interpreter—Tang Wen-sheng, Mao Tsetung, Richard Nixon and Henry Kissinger.

President Nixon announced that they would work together to establish better relations between their two countries.

In February of 1973, a year after Mr. Nixon's trip to Peking, Dr. Kissinger was back in the Chinese capital entering into further negotiations with Mao Tsetung and Chou En-lai. This time the two Chinese leaders said that though ambassadors would not be exchanged as long as the United States still recognized Taiwan, the People's Republic of China would agree to the establishment of liason offices in the capitals of both countries. These offices would perform the functions of an embassy. To all intents, the two countries would be exchanging ambassadors. Today, David K. E. Bruce heads the U.S. liason office in Peking, and Han Hsu heads the Chinese liason office in Washington, D.C.

But this was to be only a beginning. In November of 1973, Dr. Kissinger flew back to Peking to hold more discussions with Premier Chou and Chairman Mao. The goal of the leaders of both nations is eventually to establish full diplomatic relations.

China has also been reconciled with another former enemy — Japan. In September of 1972, Japanese Premier

Kakuei Tanaka went to Peking for talks with Premier Chou and Chairman Mao. At the end of the visit, the two premiers agreed to end the state of war that had existed between their countries since 1937. They signed a pact and exchanged ambassadors.

The United States and Japan are only two of the many nations with whom the People's Republic of China now has close ties of one kind or another. In 1970 she exchanged ambassadors with Canada, the first non-Communist nation in the Western Hemisphere to recognize her. Mexico quickly followed. China also now has envoys in Peru and West Germany, and has signed an extensive trade pact with Italy.

China is recognized by almost all European countries and has widened her relations with African nations. In the last ten years, she has contributed more than $1,200,000,000 to the construction of roads and factories in North Africa. And 26 per cent of the foreign aid that Peking sends abroad goes to Arab countries.

China's biggest foreign aid project, however, is the Tanzam Railway, which will eventually link the African nations of Tanzania and Zambia. More than 15,000 Chinese technicians and workers are building the railroad. Part of the construction costs are being paid for from the sale of Chinese goods to the Zambian government. China is paying the rest of the expenses.

In Southeast Asia, too, China is reasserting herself with pacts of friendship and aid in constructing roads. In the years ahead, she plans to play a more active role in world affairs. And her efforts will be bent toward taking the leadership of the Communist world away from the Soviet Union.

8

The Three Cities
of Peking

Peking, the capital of the People's Republic of China, is a magical place to Chinese everywhere. For 2,000 years off and on, it was the headquarters of many local dynasties. Then in 1260, Kublai Khan made it the capital of his Empire. And now again it is recognized as an an important city.

Peking lies on the broad flat North China plain. When winds blow out of Mongolia carrying the dust of the Gobi Desert, the bright-blue northern sky is veiled in a yellow mist. Rains come to the plain in the summer, and the weather then is so hot and humid that the people speak of it as "tiger heat days." The spring and the fall are very pleasant, but the winter is cold with light snowfalls.

To keep warm, people wear several layers of padded jackets and trousers. The Chinese describe the weather as "one-layer," "two-layer" or "three-layer" weather, depending on how many layers of clothing they have to wear to keep warm.

Peking, which has a population of about seven million people, is really three cities, one within the other. The outermost city is the modern city, with tall government buildings, factories, and three-story apartment houses.

The inner city is the old city. In its center lies the royal city, where twenty-four emperors ruled until the Manchu Dynasty was toppled by the Revolution of 1911.

The inner city was once enclosed by walls. Now most of them have been torn down to make way for modern streets, which are wide and lined with trees. The widest of the streets is Changan Avenue. In fact, it is one of the widest streets in the world. It runs from east to west, while other streets run north and south. And a chain of interconnected streets circles the whole city. Between each street are both residential and business sections.

In the older residential sections, the lanes are narrow and hemmed in by gray walls behind which lie old-style adobe houses. But in the newer sections, the streets are wider and lined with rows of new apartment houses.

The residential sections are quiet. But the business districts are full of bustle and life. There are big department stores and market places and little shops full of brightly patterned materials. The shelves of the pottery shops are filled with bowls and vases in bright colors and gay designs. In the bookshops, children and grownups alike cluster over the comic books with their Communist themes. And there are plenty of food stalls where one can stop for a cup of tea or a bean cake or a bowl of noodles.

In the heart of Peking is the royal city, or Forbidden City, as it was called because no commoner was allowed to enter uninvited. It is enclosed in wine-red walls, and each corner is topped by a golden tower. The palaces within these walls were started in 1406 by the Ming Dynasty and were added to by the Manchu Dynasty. Now they cover 250 acres of land like a sea of wooden buildings painted red and roofed with gold-glazed tiles. Today the Forbidden City is known as the Palace Museum, and it is open to everyone. There are always many visitors, but on Sunday, the only day the workers have off, the Forbidden City is very crowded.

Sunday is also a special day for twelve-year-old Tseng Pei-yuan and his sixteen-year-old sister, because that is the day their parents and baby sister come to visit them. The Tsengs, who are both engineers, work in the No. 1 Machine Tool Plant in the suburbs of Peking. The plant manufactures giant, power-operated lathes and large cutting tools, which are used in other factories to make tractors, freighters, and railroad equipment.

The Tsengs work for about ten or twelve hours a day. Now and then, when they have to solve an especially difficult problem, they stay at the plant overnight. Many of the problems the Tsengs experience are due to China's lack of money to buy new machinery and equipment. So, when a piece of machinery wears out, the Tsengs work with the factory crews figuring out ways to repair it.

This is happening in factories all over China. Sometimes, when everything else fails, the workers substitute manual labor for the equipment they lack. Then crews of men lift, carry, and set up heavy machinery, work that is usually done by cranes. Other crews, using ordinary hammers, simply beat into shape such heavy pieces of machinery as the main shafts of tractors.

The Tsengs live in a tiny apartment in one of the three-story apartment houses that have been built near the plant for the employees. The apartment buildings are set among plots of grass, trees, and bright flowers. Nearby are schools and shopping and recreation centers.

The Tsengs pay about $2 a month rent for their apartment. It has electricity and gas heating. Though it is rather bare, it is quite neat. There is a tiny living room and a small alcove into which a bed just fits. Another alcove is the kitchen. The Tsengs don't mind, since they do very little cooking at home. They usually eat at the factory canteen, where the meals are good and inexpensive. As for the bathroom, they share it with other occupants of the floor.

Only two people can live in their small apartment.

A workers' residential area.

They would have taken a larger one if the children had been staying with them. But they feel they are too busy to give their children the care they need. Instead Mr. Tseng's mother cares for the children in the old family home in the city.

The Tsengs' baby lives with them. There is a nursery school in the plant for children through kindergarten. Mrs. Tseng leaves the baby there in the morning, and gets time off during the day to nurse her. When the baby gets a little older, the Tsengs can even board her at the nursery if they wish.

Though they are separated from their children during the week, the Tsengs are fortunate—they are able to work together. Some married couples in China are separated from each other in order to work at jobs in different parts of the country. These couples see each other only several times a year. But this is accepted as the normal course of things. In the People's Republic of China, skilled technicians like the Tsengs are asked to make sacrifices for their country's welfare, and they seldom complain about it.

Before the Cultural Revolution, the Tsengs were members of their factory union, which in turn belonged to the All-China Federation of Trade Unions. The Federation was State-controlled. It never ordered the workers out on strike for higher pay. Instead, it explained government policy to the individual factory unions and relayed to them the quotas set by the State.

The individual unions held study classes in communism for their workers, and provided such things as free hospital care, nurseries for the children of working mothers, and canteens which served inexpensive meals. They also gave pensions to retired workers, and sent those who no longer had families to care for them to "homes of respect."

During the Cultural Revolution, the Federation and its unions were abolished because they had been controlled by Liu Shao-chi. In their place, revolutionary committees were set up. Today the Federation is being reorganized. The Tsengs, like every other worker in China, will have membership in it.

Mrs. Tseng also belongs to the Federation of Women. It is a political organization sponsored by the government, and was established to help women assert their rights. The organization is made up of regional committees, which send representatives to the National Committee of the Federation. The women in the Federation are urged to fight for their rights. It is part of the State's continuing campaign to get equality for them.

Although Chinese women have much more freedom than before, they are still far from the goal of complete equality. They can get an education and train to become engineers, or tractor operators, or research workers, but it is much harder for them to get work when their education is completed. Few of them ever become factory managers or hold similar positions of responsibility. They sometimes even have trouble getting jobs as factory workers. When they do, their salaries are lower than a man's, though they may do the same amount of work.

Today, though, women have a greater political voice than before. More and more of them are becoming committee members on the local level. In the higher levels of government, 17 women were elected to the 170-member Central Committee during the 1973 Tenth Congress of the Chinese Communist Party. But of the twenty-one members of the Politburo, only two are women, and one of these is Chiang Ching, the third wife of Chairman Mao. No women are represented in the powerful nine-man Standing Committee of the Politburo.

On Sunday, Mr. and Mrs. Tseng ride their bicycles into Peking, and the whole family goes on an outing for the day. Sometimes they take their lunch to one of the many parks scattered around the city, which have earned Peking the name of "garden city of the world." Often they go to the Palace Museum.

The Tsengs cross the square of Tien An Men. Once closed to the people, it has now been opened and enlarged so that it is the largest square in the world. Millions of people gather here for patriotic rallies. Parades down Changan Avenue are reviewed by Mao Tse-tung from the rostrum atop Tien An Men Gate where he announced the founding of the People's Republic.

To the left of the square rises the massive People's Hall, built of white stone. Here the National Assembly gathers when it convenes in Peking, and visiting dignitaries are treated to banquets in its huge halls.

When the Tseng family passes through Tien An Men Gate, they leave the modern world behind and slip back into the breathtaking brilliance of China's imperial past. Wine-colored archways lead through wine-colored walls. From the second archway stretches a vast courtyard divided by a waterway.

The Tseng family cross the bridges and go through

another great gateway guarded by a pair of bronze lions. Now they find themselves looking at the three principal halls of the palace complex. Built of wood, they stand one behind the other on three-tiered terraces of white marble, each terrace surrounded by a carved marble balustrade.

They are the Hall of Supreme Harmony, the Hall of Complete Harmony, and the Hall of Preserving Harmony. The Hall of Supreme Harmony, the largest, was once the throne room. It is nine stories high, and its wooden walls are painted a deep wine color, too. Its gold-glazed tile roof gleams against the blue sky. Its painted beams and bright vermilion columns glow above the white marble. Inside the hall, on a raised platform stands the throne, which is flanked on either side by six columns twined with dragons. On the ceiling high above, other gilded dragons play with huge replicas of pearls.

"It was in this hall that the emperors proclaimed their accession to the throne," Mr. Tseng tells the children. "When the emperor ascended the throne, gongs and chimes of jade sounded. Clouds of incense rose from all those bronze cranes and tortoises you see on the terraces. And there were other censors and tripods besides. Out in the courtyard, government officials and military officers knelt in rows. People like us weren't allowed inside."

To the sides and rear of the three great halls, there are many lesser halls with temples, courtyards, and towers. Gigantic carved stone animals keep guard everywhere. Finally, at the end of the Forbidden City, the Tsengs come to Chingshan Hill, which was once the Imperial Park.

When their day's outing is over, the Tsengs go to the family home, which is on Pebble Lane, one of the narrow-walled lanes in the older part of town. Gates in the walls open into courtyards lined on three sides by rooms. A few chickens who pick for food in the courtyard supply the family with eggs and sometimes, on a feast day, a chicken dinner.

In the Tseng home the rooms are shared by grandmother Tseng, Uncle Wen and Aunt Mei and their two children, Uncle Lin and Aunt Lang and their three children, and Pei-yuan and his sister. The children live together like brothers and sisters.

All the aunts and uncles work, and among them they earn about eighty dollars a month. This is a comfortable living for the Tsengs. They don't have to pay rent on the family home, and the union provides free medical care for the workers and low-cost medical care for their families. The Tsengs have been able to buy a sewing machine and two bicycles and even save a little too.

The aunts and uncles all have different jobs. Uncle Lin works eight hours a day in a state-owned watch factory. The government sells the watches in department stores or exports them to nations in Southeast Asia. Almost everyone in China today has enough money to buy a watch.

Uncle Lin eats his lunch in the factory-run lunchroom. Usually it is a heaping bowl of noodles with a little fish and vegetables, for which he pays about fifteen cents.

Aunt Lang clerks in a large department store. Once the store sold expensive dresses, furs, and other clothes to foreigners. Today it serves both city people and peasants. Its shelves are filled with Chinese clothing, cooking utensils, thermos bottles, flashlights, and farm tools. Shoppers can buy a warm jacket for two or three dollars and a vacuum flask or a small flashlight for a dollar or so.

Aunt Mei works in a little shop which she started with several other women in the lane. The women have set up their own sewing machines in an ancestral hall down the way. They make children's clothes on order for the State.

Uncle Wen teaches jade carving in a handicraft school. He learned the art from grandfather Tseng, who was a master craftsman. The techniques had been passed down from generation to generation. But Uncle Wen says they would have been lost if the People's Republic of China hadn't come to power.

Grandfather had gone so deeply into debt because of the high taxes he had to pay that he lost the jade shop. Soon afterwards he died. Uncle Wen, who had been in business

Teaching apprentices the traditional techniques of ivory carving.

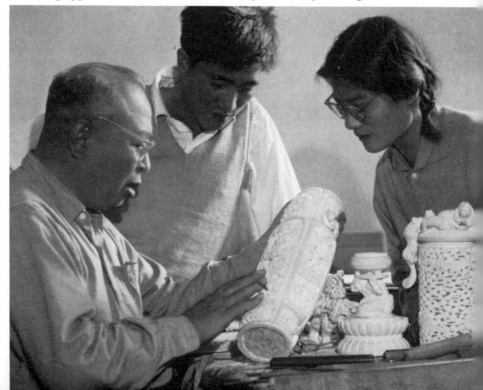

with him, had to look for other work. Sometimes he pulled rickshaws, but most of the time he begged.

When the People's Republic came to power, the government began to revive all the folk arts that had been neglected during the past years. Uncle Wen and other artisans were asked to teach what they knew to young people. Soon skilled ivory and wood carvers, and figurine, paper-cutout, and shellwork artists were teaching in handicraft schools all over China.

The art of puppeteering, which is at least two thousand years old in China, was also a dying skill until the Communists revived it. Now the children enjoy watching a puppet show in the little outdoor theater in one of Peking's many parks.

The puppets "sing" such Communist songs as "Red Flowers Turning to the Sun" and "The East Is Red." And the plays they perform are about poor peasants fighting wicked landlords.

Sometimes the whole family attends an acrobatic show in one of the big city theaters. Two thousand years ago, acrobats provided entertainment for the courts of the Han Dynasty, but then the art lost favor. Today acrobatic performers are back again, more skillful than ever.

There are ballets and operas too. Grandmother Tseng remembers the time when the operas told stories of emperors, princesses, noblemen, scholars, and villains. The stories today are about heroes and heroines from the common people. The operas have been composed by teams of writers under the supervision of Chairman Mao's wife, Chiang Ching, a former actress herself. One such opera, *The Red Detachment of Women,* tells the story of Communist women who fought in the Civil War. At the close of every opera, the cast usually sings, "Sailing the Seas Depends on the Helmsman." The helmsman is Chairman Mao, and this is a tribute to him.

The children also have fun just going with grandmother to the State Market when she shops for the family dinners. Because the market is run by the State, everything costs the same low price. They enjoy wandering around among the different stalls. Here are rows of fat green cabbages, stacks of bright orange carrots, leeks, glossy water chestnuts, and tomatoes brought in that morning from the farms outside the city. There are heaps of apples, peaches, and pears, which come from nearby orchards, and occasionally oranges from far western Szechuan. Sometimes there are great clusters of bananas or heaps of yellow papaya brought by cargo junks from Kwangtung province far to the south.

The silvery fish are so fresh that they are still quivering. Huge live crabs make ticking noises as they scramble over one another in big wicker baskets. And there are live tur-

Vegetable market inside the Chaoyangmen Gate, Peking.

keys cooped up in pens, while slabs of beef and pork and whole plucked chickens hang in rows.

"It's not like the old days," Grandmother says, as she carefully chooses the food she will prepare for dinner, and puts it in her basket. "Then all we ate was husks and wind. We couldn't afford food like this." When Grandmother speaks of eating wind, she means, of course, that they had nothing at all to eat.

Grandmother is an important person in Pebble Lane. She is a member of the Communist Party and leads a neighborhood Committee. Every neighborhood in the city has a committee made up mostly of elderly people like herself. They hold political study groups to discuss what they should do to be good Communists. Everyone in China attends such study groups. The aunts and uncles have them in the places where they work. And the children have their own study groups at school.

Grandmother and her committee members do more than just talk of ways of being a good Communist. They try to live a life of service. They make sick calls and run a little clinic where they treat the minor illnesses of neighborhood people. If the illness proves serious, they see that the person gets to one of the State hospitals, where there is free or low-cost care.

The committee also conducts classes in hygiene and sanitation. Such classes have been an important part of the education program in the People's Republic of China. They are held everywhere, in cities and villages. And they have been greatly responsible for eliminating diseases.

In the old days, people thought that devils caused diseases. So they built their houses with upturned corners on their roofs. They believed this would stop the devils, who, they were sure, flew everywhere but only in straight lines. If the devils couldn't get around the corners, they wouldn't be able to reach the chimneys and come down them to harm the family.

Because people were sure the devils preferred boy babies, they dressed the boys like girls until they were seven years old, braiding their hair and putting rings in their ears. And every child, whether boy or girl, wore the little stone figure of a lion or a red square of cloth on a string around his neck. This amulet was supposed to ward off evil influences.

Nobody realized that it was the flies that brought cholera, the rats that carried bubonic plague, contaminated water that caused typhoid, and filth that helped spread smallpox and polio. When illness struck, they just said it was the will of Heaven.

Today through the study classes they know better. Everyone gets his vaccinations and innoculations. And everyone takes part in the frequent campaigns that are waged against garbage, rats, mice, and flies.

Grandmother's committee holds many of these campaigns throughout the year. Everyone in the neighborhood helps with them, including the children. While the grown people set out traps or poison for the rats and mice, the children run up and down the lane with swatters waging war on flies. By the end of the campaign, there's scarcely a fly or a rodent to be seen.

9

School and Sports

Grandmother is the first of the family up every morning. She hurries out to the lane to join the other elderly people in her neighborhood. They gather early every morning to do some *Tai chi-chuan,* an ancient Chinese form of exercise. Each graceful movement of the *Tai chi-chuan* symbolizes some movement in nature—the elegant curve of a swan's neck, flowing water, the calm of a quiet tree. From her childhood, grandmother has been taught that performing these movements brings her into harmony with life, which is an ancient Chinese ideal.

Grandmother and her group are not the only ones to perform exercises in China. Though it is not compulsory, 90 per cent of the people start the day with exercises.

The younger people and the school children usually do modern calesthenics on the school playgrounds. Workers perform their exercises in front of the factories where they are employed. Peasants do them in the village before they go into the fields.

When grandmother has finished her exercises, she is ready to serve breakfast. In north China, where the principal crops are wheat and millet, breakfast is a bowl of noodles with some vegetables and a little fish. In south China, the bowls would contain rice, which is the principal crop there.

Grandmother ladles breakfast into bowls for the family,

Middle school pupils exercise in front of Peking Workers' Stadium.

and everyone eats with chopsticks. Then, one after the other, they hurry off to work or school. The older Tseng children go to Middle School, which is the Chinese equivalent of a high school. The younger children, including Pei-yuan, go to the Wenhsing Street Primary School. In winter, all the children dress alike in padded jackets, trousers, and high cloth boots. But in warmer weather, the older girls wear trousers and bright print blouses. Pei-yuan and his seven-year-old cousin, Ho-fei, wear shorts while ten-year-old Hu-lan wears a gay flowered dress. Children as well as grown-ups wear plastic sandals. In old China sandals were made of straw or cloth, but plastic lasts longer.

In the early morning hours, the streets are filled with thousands of people on bicycles on their way to work. The air rings with the noise of bicycle bells, the honking of bus horns, and the clanging of streetcar bells. The few automobiles are used only for official business. Though China manufacturers cars, they would be much too expensive for ordinary people. But almost everyone owns a bicycle.

This is the time, too, for peasants to bring their produce into the State Markets. Long processions of mules and horses draw wagons loaded with vegetables, fruit, pigs, chickens, and grain. Peasants pedal three-wheeled pedicabs filled with vegetables. A horse-drawn truck moves slowly up the street as the crew collects the garbage. It will be taken out to the country, where it will be used to make fertilizer.

Wherever the children look, they do not see any beggars. There is plenty of work and enough to eat for everyone, and the government permits no one to be idle. Any beggar would quickly find himself in a labor camp to be re-educated in Communism.

By seven-forty, the children arrive at the Wenhsing Street Primary School. On one wall of the four story red brick building, giant white Chinese characters read, "Study well and make progress every day." It is one of Mao Tsetung's sayings.

On the school grounds, the teachers are helping the children form lines. Most of the teachers are young women, but the athletic instructors are men.

Suddenly the blare of a bugle comes over a loud speaker. A commanding voice recites a quote from Chairman Mao: "Promote physical culture and build up the people's health." Then lively music begins. From the speaker a voice calls, "One . . . two . . . three . . . four . . ." And the children perform calesthenics, jumping, bending, twisting, and turning in brisk rhythm.

After five minutes of exercising, the children go into the

classrooms. They attend school six days a week and get only Sunday off. Classes begin at 8 A.M. and last until three.

Education in China isn't free, but the fees are so low that all parents can afford to send their children. It amounts to about $2.50 a year for tuition, books, and supplies.

The children are given courses in Chinese language, music, drawing, political science, history, fine arts, agriculture, and industry. Beginning with the third grade, the students at Wenhsing Street school study English. In other schools they can learn French, Spanish, or German.

In middle school, the courses also include physics, chemistry, and biology. Almost everything the children study has a political flavor, and they learn the importance of serving the masses as a good Communist.

At the end of each term, the children receive report cards. During the Cultural Revolution, the school stopped giving grades, but they found that this caused school standards to drop. Now the teachers not only give grades but also comment on the child's over-all progress. The commentary describes the child's attitude toward his work, studies, schoolmates, and teachers.

At the end of the year, if a student fails one major or two minor subjects, he has to repeat the year. But this doesn't happen often, because the children try to help one another with their studies.

Children get more than an academic education. One week out of every term, they go to a city factory. For example, at the Peking Pharamceutical Company's Plant No. 2, which makes drugs, the children help the workers by washing jars, packing medicines, and making boxes. Once a term, they are taken outside the city to a Commune, where they help the peasants weed their fields, harvest their crops, or water their vegetable gardens. Every week, army men give them military training. All the classes turn out on the playground wearing red and white uniforms, belts, and Mao badges. They march and perform rifle drills with wooden guns.

They have two vacations a year, the month of January and the month of July. Their vacations are arranged by teachers and street and factory committees.

Most schools in China follow the pattern of the Wenh-sing school, but there are some differences. In south China, where the climate is subtropical and often very warm, children start school at 7:40 A.M., but go home for lunch and a rest that lasts from 11 A.M. to 2:30 P.M. Then they return to school until four.

Some schools have workshops of their own. Instructors from nearby factories come several times a week to show the children how to assemble radios or television sets. Everything the children make in their workshop will be bought by

A group and its director help out in a neighborhood factory.

the State, and the money received will be used to improve their school. Even the little second graders do their share, removing cork from bottle caps to be used again.

In some schools, a peasant instructor comes once a week to give the children a course in farming. In country schools, the children learn about farming by growing their own vegetables in a garden plot near the school. Several times a year, when the vegetables ripen, the children have a feast prepared for them by the teachers from the things they have grown.

In other schools, particularly in the country, children are served an "eat bitterness" meal several times a year. The meal is made up of husks and wild root gruel, which was the only food many poor peasants had before the founding of the People's Republic of China. Afterwards an old peasant describes the hard times he suffered when he was young. These lessons are given to make the students realize how much they owe the People's Republic of China, and to inspire them to work enthusiastically for their country.

Schools in the country are generally not as large or as well staffed as those in the city, and the parents pay even lower fees for their children's tuition. In the poorest sections of the country, the school is just one room in a small adobe building where the teacher, usually a teen-ager, handles all grades at once. The children's desks and benches are made of adobe, fashioned by their parents.

In some places, classes are held without a classroom. In the early morning, the young cowherders of the Yangtze River delta region take their cows out to graze. With them is a young teen-ager, a high school graduate, carrying blackboard, chalk, and a little red book of Mao's thought. While the cows graze, he teaches the children arithmetic, writing the problems on the board. He will teach reading and political lessons from the little red book.

Most of the big cities and larger towns have recreation centers for the children. There are several of these Children's Palaces in Peking. Three times a week after school, Pei-yuan and Hu-lan go to the one nearest their home. It gives special classes in drawing, clay modeling, dancing, or experimenting with model rocket ships.

Hu-lan has joined a little orchestra made up of young girls. Some of their instruments are modern, such as flutes, brass horns, and drums. Others date back to ancient China. These are the large banjolike pipa, the smaller, stringed guchin, and the sheng, a kind of mouth organ. With this assortment of instruments, the children learn to play "The East Is Red," the national anthem of the People's Republic of China.

On other afternoons, they busy themselves with activities in the Red Guard organization. Though the militant Red Guard was disbanded after the Cultural Revolution, it has now been reorganized along peaceful lines. The Middle School students are called Red Guards. The primary grade students are called Little Red Soldiers and wear red kerchiefs around their necks.

The Red Guards and Little Red Soldiers serve their community in many ways. They take turns going to school at seven in the morning to clean up their classrooms and prepare things for the day. They write the school newspaper, which is made up of blackboards set out on the school yard. The children write Communist slogans, along with stories about students who have served the people in some special way. Each morning, they erase the boards and write something new.

The Middle School students also give their time in clinics and visit shut-ins. Some of them form theatrical troupes that entertain the peasants in the country or the workers in city factories. The songs they sing and the shows they put on all have Communist themes.

The Little Red Soldiers also have theatrical troupes, and they too perform many services. Pei-yuan and Hu-lan and several other neighborhood children sweep their lane clean. They check on the neighbors to be sure that garbage is being left for the trucks instead of being dumped in the lane.

Seven-year-old Ho-fei and some of his classmates direct traffic. The children stand on little platforms in the middle of street intersections to help patrol the cyclists. Some of the cyclists pay no attention to the signs and run right through the stop signals.

Traffic tickets are not given in China. But the children often scold violators through their megaphones. Everyone around laughs and applauds, and the cyclist rides off in embarrassment.

In the cold winter after the snowfalls, there is always plenty of work for everyone, Red Guards and Little Red Soldiers included. Early in the morning, thousands of people clear the streets of snow and ice. Using brooms, hoes, and shovels, they sweep away the loose white snow and chip at the hard ice underneath. Occasionally water trucks come by, spraying hot steam on the streets to make the work easier.

There is a lot of work in the fall, too, because it is house-cleaning time in Peking. Everybody scrubs floors, sweeps courtyards, and brushes away cobwebs. The older children whitewash the walls of their homes, inside and out, as well as the courtyard walls.

Battalions of Red Guards and Little Red Soldiers sweep

and weed the courtyards in the Forbidden City and in front of the Temple of Heaven, which stands in the southern section of Peking. In the old days, emperors in chariots drawn by elephants journeyed from the palace across Peking to perform their spring sacrifices at the temple. Today it is a museum.

Autumn, with its soaring winds, is kite-flying season. The kite makers in the market place are busy filling orders for adults and children. These artisans have passed their skills down through generations. Sometimes after school, the Tseng children, along with hundreds of others, hurry to the square of Tien An Men. The huge square is a perfect place to fly a kite. Soon gay silken butterflies, tadpoles, dragons, and feathered hawk shapes are swooping and dancing against the sun.

The Wenshing Street Primary School has two recesses, one in the morning and one in the afternoon. During these periods the children are encouraged to take part in sports. It is all part of Chairman Mao's directive, "Promote physical culture and build up the people's health."

Pei-yuan usually spends his recess playing basketball. Hu-lan likes to jump rope, and Ho-fei enjoys ping-pong. For the children who stay after school, there is usually a football or basketball game, with the coaches acting as referees.

Most schools now devote at least one hour a day to sports, and many are organizing athletic meets in swimming, track, basketball, football, and ping-pong. Though the sports are competitive, the children are taught not to be concerned solely with winning.

"Friendship first, competition second," is the motto. If winning a game means losing a friend, it is better to lose the game.

Children who excel in athletics are sent to Physical Training Institutes to get special coaching. In Peking, they go to the Youth Amateur Athletic School, which was established in 1958. The school has more than fifty coaches and one thousand students between the ages of seven and sixteen.

Hu-lan is one of the pupils. Like all the children who attend, she was selected on the recommendation of her teacher. Three times a week, she is excused from primary school for the afternoon to attend classes at the Athletic School. She is learning *wushu,* the ancient and very difficult art of swordplay.

For the past two years, Hu-lan has been practicing basic body-building exercises to improve her physique. Today she is very agile, and her form is almost always correct as she twirls or holds upright or extends her broad sword with the gay red tassel swinging from its handle. Dressed in red and white costumes, she and her classmates often spend their holidays putting on exhibitions for workers and peasants.

Besides *wushu,* the coaches in the Youth Amateur Athletic School teach such sports as basketball, volleyball, track, and ping-pong. The coaches also give gymnastic classes in factories and outlying schools. Thousands of the school's graduates have become physical education teachers.

But sports aren't only for children and young people. Everyone in China is encouraged to participate. One of the big events in Peking is the annual Peking City Race. It has been taking place during the Spring Festival in February ever since 1956. Starting at the great square of Tien An Men, the runners go completely around the city and back to the starting point. There are no prizes for the winners, but the honor is great. And every year some three thousand men, women, and teen-agers from Peking and the surrounding communes enter the race. Most of them begin their training four months in advance.

Another big event is the track-and-field meet held in June at the Peking Workers' Stadium. Athletes from all over the country gather there to race, high jump, and throw the discus. But instead of competing, they coach one another in the sports in which they excel. After the meet, troupes of athletes tour the countryside putting on meets and coaching the peasants in basketball and ping-pong. This is part of their policy of serving the people by sharing their skills. The Chinese people have high regard for their athletes. However, the athletes themselves are taught that they are no better than any other worker in China, and must share what they learn with others.

The price of admission to all sporting events is about thirty cents, but tickets are hard to get because the events are very popular. All the seats are taken even before an advertisement appears in the Communist paper, *The People's World,* or a single wall poster goes up.

Ping-pong tournaments are especially popular. The game has become the most widespread sport in the People's Republic of China. Almost everyone plays. The Chinese say it is a true people's sport because it is inexpensive and so is within the reach of everyone.

Ping-pong tournaments have been used to promote friendship with the people of other nations. Foreign teams are often invited to China, and the Chinese team tours other countries. An American team was invited to play a tournament in China even before President Nixon's visit. The matches take place indoors at the Peking Capital Stadium. It seats eighteen thousand people and is so large that twenty-four games can be played at the same time.

The foreign teams are treated to more than games. Troupes of primary and high school students in colorful costumes entertain them with peasant folk dances and pageants of welcome. The guests are taken on tours of the Great Wall and the Forbidden City, and they are given banquets in the People's Hall. China hopes that when the teams go back to their countries, they will spread good will for the People's Republic of China.

 **10**

Other Cities

Peking is only one of the many important Chinese cities. Each city has a different flavor because China is such a large country. Her territory extends from the frozen lands of the Northeast Region to the tropical island of Hainan some 2,500 miles to the south.

The Northeast Region is rich in coal and iron. Soon after the Japanese began occupying the region in 1905, they started developing these minerals. Over the years, three sister cities —Mukden, Anshan, and Fushun—sprang up in the southern plain of the region. These cities have been rapidly expanding under the People's Republic of China.

Mukden, called Shenyang by the Chinese, is an ancient city. It was the first capital of the Manchus before they invaded China, and some of their emperors are buried here. Today it is a bustling industrial center with factories, textile mills, and machine tool shops.

The coal needed to power the factories in Shenyang comes from nearby Fushun, where beds of rich coal lie under layers of earth. Coal from Fushun has been dug for so many years that today the mine is the largest open pit in the world. The houses of the town rim the pit.

Anshan is the site of China's largest iron-smelting plant. The iron ore taken from mines in the vicinity is processed into pig iron and steel. This raw material is sent to the factories of Shenyang as well as to other industrial cities.

A coal mine at Fushun.

China's largest city is still Shanghai, which has become more and more industrialized. Today it has a population of ten million people.

The massive buildings and skyscrapers built by the foreigners give the Whangpoo River shoreline a western look. But the flavor of old China still remains in the narrow streets and alleyways that were once the native quarter.

Much of the slum area has been cleared away, but rebuilding continues. It takes a very long while to remake a city as large as Shanghai. Many people still live on narrow lanes in tiny adobe houses with dirt or stone floors. In some of these neighborhoods, there is no running water. Water still has to be drawn from the community pump. But there is electricity for everyone, even though people use it sparingly—usually one lightbulb to a house.

Though Shanghai is one of China's largest industrial cities, she has no resources of her own. The raw materials have to be brought from other places. The pig iron and steel are shipped down the Yangtze from the iron-mining center of Maanshan or from Anshan, in the far north. The coal comes from North China. And the oil for Shanghai's oil refinery is carried by train from Sinkiang, far to the west.

Shanghai has one valuable asset—thousands of skilled workers. Some of them are employed in the shipyards. China has already manufactured six 10,000-ton freighters, and more are on the way.

In the large steel plant, workers smelt more than 5,000 tons of steel a day. And the many factories around the city produce such things as electronic equipment, machine tools, chemicals, plastics, textiles, and radios. Some of these articles are sold at home. Others are exported to Southeast Asia and Africa.

Shanghai's new factories are located in the suburbs, where space isn't a problem. Around each factory there is a residential district of three-story apartment houses surrounded by grass and shade trees. Each housing unit has its own schools, shopping and recreation centers, hospital, and "home of respect" for retired workers.

Up the Yangtze River from Shanghai stands another of China's large industrial centers. It is the city of Wuhan located where the Yangtze and Han rivers meet in the Middle Yangtze plain. Wuhan is really three cities—Wuchang, Hankow, and Hanyang. Wuchang, which stands on the south bank of the Yangtze, is an ancient walled town and cultural center with a large medical and agricultural university in its suburbs.

Hankow was built by the British in the 1800s. There is an English atmosphere about the massive Victorian-style buildings that line the riverfront. But behind them lies a maze of alleyways hemmed in by two-story wooden shacks. Some of the shacks are so old that they lean sideways and have large gaps between the planks of their board walls.

In the hot summertime, the people of Hankow move out of their stuffy houses into the street. They cook, eat, and wash clothes outside. And at night, they bring out their bed mats to sleep under the stars.

Many of the people who live in Hankow work in the big steel plant in Hanyang, the third of the cities. This is the steel plant that the Russians abandoned in 1960. Chinese engineers have long since finished and expanded it, but the bitterness toward the Russians still remains. The Chinese look on it as a kind of betrayal.

Today the plant is the second largest in China. Sixty-five thousand workmen operate the four blast furnaces and thirteen mills that turn out steel. Neighboring factories use the steel to manufacture heavy machine tools, diesel engines, electric motors, tractors, and ball bearings.

Despite China's growing industrialization, much of the old country still remains. The quiet flavor of past centuries can be felt in the flat countryside that stretches away south from Shanghai. This is the famous Water Country, so called because it contains many lakes, canals, ponds, and streams caused by the heavy rainfall.

Small towns and villages line the waterways, which serve as the main transportation routes. Processions of barges heaped with rice, vegetables, pigs, chickens, and cotton move down the canals from country communes to the State-owned marketplaces.

Flocks of ducks swim peacefully. And blue-jacketed women squat on the stone steps that lead down from their front doors to the water. They wash their clothes here, pounding and beating them with wooden sticks to loosen the dirt.

Sometimes men fish from little rafts, but they do not fish in the regular way. On each raft sits a cormorant, which has been tamed and trained by its owner. When the bird sees a fish in the water, he dives for it. But a string or a copper ring around the big bird's neck keeps it from swallowing the fish. He brings it back to the raft, and the fisherman drops it in a basket. Later he will sell his fish to a State-owned marketplace.

The ancient Grand Canal, which has been widened and deepened in recent years, cuts through the water country connecting two of the most beautiful cities in China. One is Soochow, which stands on the bank of the Canal; the other is Hangchow, which lies at its southern end.

For centuries the Chinese have called these cities "Heaven on Earth," and both were favorite resorts of the emperors. Today thousands of Chinese tourists visit the cities.

Industry has passed by Soochow, but it has come to Hangchow. For years the little town which stands on the shores of beautiful West Lake, was known mainly for its scenic charm. Its chief exports were its flavorful tea, which is grown on the terraced hills nearby, and its silk brocade fabrics made from the silk of locally cultivated silkworms.

Today chemical fertilizer plants, machine tool factories and small iron and steel works have sprung up in its wooded suburbs. They are hidden from sight and do not spoil the rustic loveliness of the little resort. Only occasionally do telltale plumes of smoke reveal the presence of a growing industry.

Below Hangchow, on the banks of the Pearl River, stands the largest city in south China. The Chinese call it Kwangchow, but in the Western world it is known as Canton. It has a population of 2,200,000 people and is surrounded by rich agricultural country. All around the city are green fields of rice, dotted with ponds and cut with canals and rivulets. Here and there, a low rolling hill rises like an island out of the green sea.

Canton is a carefree city. Its marketplace is decorated with gay streamers and banners bearing Communist slogans. The people who swarm down its narrow streets have a jaunty air about them. They are shorter and far more wiry than the tall northern Chinese. They speak in a sharp staccato dialect, which is so different from that of Peking. As a result, southerners and northerners can't understand one another.

There are a great number of dialects in China, perhaps

as many as two thousand. Most of them are in the south, where rugged mountain ranges prevent people from moving around easily. Often the villages in neighboring valleys can't understand one another.

The Chinese government is trying to unite the country under the Peking or Mandarin dialect because it is the most frequently spoken in China. So, in most primary schools in the south, students are being taught their lessons in Mandarin.

Meanwhile, the only means of communication between the different parts of China is through written characters. These characters, which the Chinese use instead of letters, are uniform all over the country.

In Canton, industrial growth has been much slower than in the north because of the lack of coal and iron resources. But there are some sugar refineries, which process the raw sugar cane that grows in the delta, and mills to make paper out of the sugar cane pulp. There are also cement, fertilizer, and chemical plants and a large bicycle factory.

These are only some of China's industrial cities. There are others. Loyang, on the Yellow River, makes tractors. In Chungking located on the Yangtze River behind the gorges, electrical equipment and machine tools are made. Tientsin, which is Peking's seaport, manufactures tractors, bicycles, and diesel engines. All these cities are expanding, and many others are springing up as China enters the industrial age.

Industrialization means pollution, and the Chinese have been growing more and more aware of the problem. In Peking, heavy industry has been restricted to the east and south suburbs. The winds come from a north-northwest direction, and this keeps much of the smog away from the city. But there is still a smoky haze on hot still days.

In Wuhan, Anshan, and especially Shanghai, factories belch noxious fumes into the air. In many industrial cities, poisonous wastes dumped into streams and lakes have already killed fish and plant life.

Today factory workers and scientific teams are cooperating to devise inexpensive and effective methods for trapping and reusing the poisonous chemicals being discharged into the air. Huge purification vats are being constructed to treat the polluted waste water from factories and then return it to the countryside for irrigation.

The Chinese people feel that they have an advantage over more fully industrialized countries in fighting pollution. By observing the mistakes other nations have made, they say, they have a better chance of keeping their air clean.

 **11**

The Countryside

Outside Peking, the wide green fields of the Chinese-Vietnamese Friendship People's Commune stretch away to the horizon. There is the lighter green of rice and the darker green of wheat, soybean, and corn. Through the fields run tree-lined roads.

In the old days, graveyards covered wide stretches of valuable farm land all over China. When people died, their families would go to soothsayers, or fortune tellers, for advice on the best place to bury their dead. It was believed that burying someone in the wrong place would bring bad luck to the living. After studying the situation, the soothsayer would select a spot. Unfortunately, the site he chose was often right in the center of a field. Then the farmers would have to plow around the graves.

Bit by bit, as there were more and more graveyards, good agricultural land was taken up. It took the *kan-pu* a long time to persuade the peasants that these graves, many of which were centuries old, could be safely removed. Now most of them are gone.

The little wayside shrines are gone too. The *kan-pu* have convinced most of the peasants that there are no nature gods—in fact, no God at all. "Man's will, not Heaven's, decides," they say.

About 38,000 people live in the Chinese-Vietnamese Friendship People's Commune, which covers thirty-eight square miles. This commune is a particularly prosperous one. It is made up of thirty-five villages, which are organized into six brigades. The brigades are divided into ninety-five production teams, each with its own work to do.

The headquarters of the commune is in the village of Shih Ken Chuang. Shih Ken Chuang hasn't changed much since the old days. The tile-roofed houses are very small, usually with two rooms apiece. Inside, in a prominent place, every home displays a large portrait of Mao Tsetung. In a corner of the room, there may be a new bicycle or a sewing machine. The family bed is still a *kang,* a brick platform built over an oven. In the winter the peasants build a fire in the oven every night, and with a blanket over them, they keep very warm.

There isn't any plumbing in the village. Instead, in a corner of each kitchen stands a huge jar which has been filled with water brought from a nearby community well by bucket. A dipper beside the jar is used to ladle out water for cooking and washing. Because electrical power is low, there is only one lightbulb in the house, and it is in the kitchen.

Almost every village has its own primary school, taught by young Middle School graduates. And every brigade has a Middle School. In every village, there is also a medical clinic where minor illnesses are treated. If someone has a serious ailment, he or she is sent to the big hospital at the commune headquarters or to a nearby big-city hospital.

The peasants don't lack for entertainment. However, almost all of it, whether in country or city, is concerned with keeping the people from slipping back into the old ways. For a few pennies a month, they can have a loudspeaker installed in their home, over which they will hear music and news reports. Traveling propaganda troupes tour the countryside, putting on free performances of operas and plays based on the revolution. Several times a week the villagers attend political study groups.

Though life is much better for the peasant today, he still is not so well off as the city worker. The city worker is paid set wages. The peasant's share of money is figured out by work points. No matter how many work points he has, if the harvest is poor his share will be cut. And, as in the cities, the women receive the smallest share, even though they do the same amount of work as the men.

Even though the Chinese-Vietnamese Friendship People's Commune is a prosperous one, it has only forty-five tractors and seventeen trucks to be shared by all thirty-five villages. So mules and horses have to be used to get the plowing done. Sometimes, when there is not enough equipment or animals available to harvest the crops, the people themselves pull the iron plows.

By pooling their resources, the commune has been able to accomplish many things. It has large dairies, pig farms, cattle and horse farms, and duck yards. Specialized production teams devote all their time to improving the animals through breeding, so they can get a higher price from the State.

Other scientific experiment groups develop strains of plants that not only stand up against cold and drought, but will also provide a bigger harvest. Still other groups work on efficient insecticides and fertilizers.

Many of the brigades have their own food-processing plants, and the commune runs a farm tool factory. In the idle winter seasons, the peasants work in the factories, earning more money for themselves and their communes.

All over China, communes are being urged to utilize the peasants spare time and improve their living conditions by putting up factories. Some of the factories are little more than handicraft shops where housewives make everything from glass and crockery to hand-woven rugs and bamboo utensils. Others are huge factory complexes that manufacture electric pumps, tractors, trucks, and other heavy farm equipment.

However, all the communes aren't equal in wealth. The rich communes are not required to help the poor ones because, under Chinese Communism, each unit is supposed to be self-sufficient. To achieve this sometimes takes backbreaking effort for a number of years.

Sandstone Hollow was such a community. It is a brigade in a poor commune located in the mountains just south of the Great Wall. Twenty-five years ago it was a desolate rocky land where seventy-eight families could scarcely scratch out a living for themselves. Most of them were forced to beg in the towns during part of the year.

When the People's Republic was established, life became very different for the peasants of Sandstone Hollow. They were urged to help themselves, since they would not get help from anyone else.

First, with their pickaxes they made 5,700 holes in the solid rock floor of Wolf's Den canyon. They filled the holes with earth carried in baskets from the upper mountain slopes. Then they planted apple trees.

Next they removed the rocks from the fields in their valley. They notched broad terraces in the rockbound lower slopes of the mountains and built stone walls around the rims of the terraces. They brought more basketloads of earth to fill the basins and planted the terraces with millet.

Now they had more fields. But they needed more water. To catch the summer rains, they built a reservoir and chiseled out twenty-five large cisterns from the rocky ground. Then, one year, a drought dried up the water supply, and most of their crop was lost. To prevent this from happening again, the people searched until they found a large spring on the far side of the mountain.

They dug a well at the spring, and with their savings, collected during good years, they bought an electric pump and some iron pipes. They installed the pump at the well and piped the water over the mountain. Today Sandstone Hollow is flourishing. The harvests from the fields meet State quotas, and every autumn there is a fine crop of apples from the orchard.

The people of Minchiao Commune had a different proba.

b.

The boulder-covered mountain slopes of Sandstone Hollow.

Removing part of a cliff.

c.

d.

Digging out the terraces.

Rock walls enclose the terraces.

e.

Transporting earth from the other side of the mountain.

f.

The earth is spread over the rock floor.

Barren slopes transformed into terraced fields.

g.

lem. This very small commune, located in the mountains of Chekiang province, is primarily a tea-growing community. In earlier days, the people did everything by hand. After they picked the young green tea leaves, they spread them out in baskets, which they rotated over slow fires to toast the leaves smoothly. It was a long, tiring job which kept production down.

However, hydroelectric power would provide the people with enough power to run factories for processing the tea. So they all got together to build a dam and an electric station on the turbulent river that ran through their commune.

First they had to widen the ravine through which the river flowed. They began in midwinter, when there was no work to be done on the small fields. Snow began to fall, but that didn't stop them. They broke the frozen ground with pickaxes. Then, while some brigades shoveled the earth away, others carried it elsewhere in baskets and bags to be dumped. Often big rocks had to be blasted out of the earth and carried away too.

After the ravine was widened, the people built the dam and a power station by hand. It took almost a year to finish, but today Minchiao has two tea-processing factories. Only twenty-one people are needed to run them. They do the work that 250 people did before. As a result, more members of the commune are free to clear more land for rice fields and to plant a large tree farm for much-needed lumber.

Though each commune acts as an independent unit, there are times when a number of communes band together to tackle huge flood control projects that will benefit the whole area. Such a project was begun eight years ago in Hopei province and is still going on. It is called the Hai

Ho River Control Project.

The Hai Ho is a short river that runs from Tientsin to the Pohai Sea. It is the outlet for five major rivers that cross Hopei Province from the Taihang Mountains to the west. For many years, these rivers have been overflowing their banks during the summer rainy season and ruining the farmlands. Then, in the dry spring season, when water is badly needed, there is none.

If the banks of the rivers were raised, the fields could be saved at flood times. If reservoirs were dug, the water could be stored for the dry season. If canals were made, they could lead the water to lands never before cultivated. This was a big dream, and it would take a lot of planning and effort, since the peasants' only tools were simple hoes and spades.

Yet there were thousands of people, and together they could do the job. The peasants worked through the long hard winters when the fields were lying fallow and didn't need care. In gales and cold, freezing sleet and snows, they chiseled away at the frozen ground, dug canals, and raised the dykes. Bit by bit, they built dams and reservoirs, bridges and sluices.

The city people of Tientsin and Peking pitched in too. Brigades of factory workers, professional people, and children joined the peasants. Together they began digging the Yungting Canal, the Peking sewage drainage channel, and a flood-prevention project on the outskirts of Peking.

All over China, similar projects are going on. Little by little, floods are being curbed, and so droughts are losing their power to harm. Wastelands are being reclaimed, and harvests have increased.

12

Doctors
and Medicine

The People's Republic of China has a number of outstanding universities. Tsinghua University in Peking is the country's largest science and engineering institute. Peking University, which was once a liberal arts institution, is now becoming an engineering school too. There are also agricultural, medical, pharmaceutical, and engineering schools in such cities as Shanghai, Nanking, Wuchang, and Canton.

Medical schools are particularly important to China. When the Communists came into power in 1949, there were only eight medical colleges in China and 20,000 doctors. By 1964, the Communists had boosted the number of medical colleges to eighty, and there were 450,000 doctors, surgeons, dentists, nurses, and other medical workers.

The doctors of the People's Republic are well trained and rank among the best in the world. They perform open heart surgery, as well as brain and lung operations. And they have been among the first to sew back severed limbs successfully.

There still aren't nearly enough doctors to take care of China's 700,000,000 people. During the Cultural Revolution, the Red Guards forced the doctors to shorten medical schooling to a two-year course that concentrated on practical experience in the operating room. The students were then sent into the countryside to perform simple operations, such as removing appendixes and treating common illnesses. Since then, however, the training period has been increased to three and a half years to ensure better doctors.

During the past few years, doctors have been training young peasants in practical nursing so they could open clinics in their home villages. These trained peasants are called "barefoot doctors" because peasants so often go barefoot. Today barefoot doctors conduct health campaigns in their own villages. They give vaccinations and innoculations and teach hygiene and birth control methods to keep China's already huge population from increasing. Even now, scarcely enough food can be raised to feed it.

There are some medical practices in China that are different from those elsewhere in the world. For example, acupuncture and the use of herbal remedies date back

A "barefoot doctor" examining a child.

hundreds of years. But Chinese doctors trained in Western medicine frowned on these traditional methods. They had very little faith in the art of acupuncture.

In acupuncture, slender silver needles are inserted into key parts of the body and then twirled. Patients claimed this treatment cured them, but the Western-trained doctors believed it was all in their imagination. Gradually, however, they began to realize that patients actually were being helped.

During the Cultural Revolution, the doctors took to heart Mao Tsetung's statement, "Make the past serve the present," and started seriously studying acupuncture. They soon found that it did have many valid uses. When the needles were inserted into various areas of the body, numbness could be produced in other areas. This meant that acupuncture could be used as an anesthetic that caused no side effects. Soon Western-style Chinese doctors were using acupuncture.

Then they discovered that acupuncture was a good treatment for such illnesses as arthritis and headaches. By experimenting on himself, Chao Pu-yu, a young medical orderly, discovered that acupuncture needles could restore the hearing of some deaf children. Today acupuncture is a standard treatment for pupils in schools for the deaf in China.

The number of drug firms in China has increased in the past twenty years from two to forty. But Western-trained doctors are no longer limiting themselves to modern drugs in the treatment of disease. They are also showing a deep interest in Chinese traditional medicine. Teams of doctors have collected thousands of herbal prescriptions from old peasants. These remedies are tested, improved upon, and then made into pills, powders, ointments, or solutions. The staffs of some hospitals have gathered herbs in the mountains and are growing them in nearby plots of ground. Experiments with these herbs are continuing all the time. They will enable barefoot doctors in isolated regions to treat many minor ailments with prescriptions they can make up themselves from the herbs in their locality.

Many of the remote regions of China have never been visited by doctors before, and the people know nothing about modern health practices. So teams of physicians, young medical school graduates, and nurses are visiting these places to treat the peasants, train barefoot doctors, and teach hygiene.

The medical teams are giving special attention to south China, where many people suffer from serious tropical diseases. One of these diseases is snail fever, which is caused by a parasite that lives in a water snail. About 200,000,000 people in various parts of the world come down with snail fever. In China, peasants get it from walking barefoot in rice paddy fields. Another serious disease is malaria, which is carried by some mosquitoes. They also breed in water.

Because of the warm climate and heavy rainfall, the villages are often breeding ground for disease. Lanes are mud ruts strewn with garbage and manure, and they swarm with flies and maggots. There are many stagnant ponds and ditches.

The people in the isolated villages of China's mountainous southwest region are still ignorant about the cause of disease. They do not know that filth breeds it.

Before they can teach these people, the doctors have to win their confidence. Often they camp in the region for several months, visiting all the nearby villages. They treat illnesses until the people learn to trust them. Then they give lectures on hygiene. From among the most capable peasants in each village, they train one or two to be barefoot doctors.

Finally the doctors persuade the villagers to have clean-up campaigns. Going from village to village, they organize work crews to fill in ponds and ditches and clear up the streets. They get the peasants to move the pig sties and animal pens away from the village. And they help them clean and purify their drinking-water tanks.

Insecticides are sprayed everywhere to kill flies and mosquitoes. But the snails are still a difficult problem. They have to be collected by hand, thousands of them, and buried in the earth. When the medical team leaves, it promises that another team will be back next year.

Only the dedication of Chinese doctors keeps them going. They will tell you that their dedication has been inspired in large part by a Canadian Communist doctor named Norman Bethune. During the war with Japan, Dr. Bethune joined the Red Army in Shensi Province. He cared for wounded soldiers in medical outposts just behind the front lines. Dr. Bethune risked his life many times before he contracted blood poisoning and died. Today the Chinese, including Chairman Mao, give him the highest praise their country can bestow. They call him a People's Hero.

A health worker shows commune members the different medicinal plants, and explains what they can do in treating and preventing diseases.

13

The People's Liberation Army

China's armed forces are still called the People's Liberation Army (PLA). They haven't changed very much since they were first organized on Chingkangshan Mountain in 1927. The rules that were set down then are still in force today. The emphasis is on service rather than military glory. It is considered an honor to be a member of the PLA, and families are proud to have their children in it.

Families of soldiers can be recognized in several ways. Nailed on the right-hand side of the front gateway of their house is a yellow wooden tablet eight inches long. Bright red characters printed on it read, "Glorious Army Family." On Army Day, August 1, as well as other national holidays, they are honored at mass meetings. High officials in their commune or city pay them visits to inquire about their health and wish them well.

Both young men and women between the ages of eighteen and twenty-two can apply for army service. They are carefully screened to be sure their physical health and political attitudes are acceptable. Recruits usually serve from three to five years, but they may stay longer. Altogether there are about 3,000,000 men and women in the Army, Navy, and Air Force of the PLA.

113

A unit stationed near the coastline of Shantung province is one of many that patrol the sea approaches to China. The men live in brick barracks near a commune. In baggy green uniforms with a red star on their caps, they are a familiar sight to their peasant neighbors. They help them dig irrigation ditches and build new canals and dams. They also hold political sessions with them.

Several times a week, the soldiers train the people of the commune. Almost everyone in China receives military training and belongs to the People's Militia. In case of invasion, the militia will fight at the side of the PLA to defend China.

Whenever possible, PLA units try to cultivate their own farms so they will be self-sufficient and not be a drain on the peasants among whom they live. The Shantung unit has reclaimed former coastal waterlands and planted millet.

The commanding officer works side by side with his men. There is nothing in his uniform or his title to distinguish him from a private. He is called "comrade" by his men, a term in common use all over China today. The CO does his share of working in the kitchen, the pig pens, the vegetable gardens, and the repair shops, where the soldiers mend their own clothing.

Many of the PLA units patrol the remote frontiers that separate China from Soviet Siberia. One of these units is located in the towering mountains above Sinkiang province. In a small clearing stand some barracks built by construction workers for the soldiers. The soldiers themselves dug a little canal to bring water to the clearing. They terraced the mountain slope and planted vegetables. Then they built a barn in which they raised pigs and chickens. Finally they brought in cattle, horses, and sheep which

A PLA telephone squad.

could graze on the mountain slopes. By the third winter, they had become almost self-sufficient.

On the opposite side of the country, the frozen Northeast Region, there is a telephone squad made up of six young PLA women. they serve as the signal company stationed on the China-Siberia border. Their duty is to keep the lines in working order. Since they are part of the Army, they also go on military maneuvers.

The PLA is giving women the same opportunities and responsibilities as men. Recently a whole class of young women pilots was graduated from the Army flying school forming China's first, and perhaps the world's first all-women flight squadron.

In the spirit of service, every PLA headquarters has its own hospital, which not only serves the armed forces but also the surrounding community. The army hospital in

Lanchow, in far western Kansu province, sends out medics who treat the widely scattered Mongolian herdsmen living along the fringes of the Gobi desert.

There are no highways in this wilderness, so the medics have to travel by camel over the desolate sand dunes and through vast barren areas. Sometimes the medic has to cure a fever, help with the birth of a baby, or perhaps set a broken arm or leg.

The herdsmen had never received such care before. Now the devotion of the medics whom the herdsmen call "Our Gobi Desert Hospital on Camelback," has done much to bring the Mongolians and Chinese closer after centuries of mistrust and warfare.

The Cultural Team, which forms a part of the Lanchow PLA unit, is also working to heal old rifts. Traveling across the high lonely wastes of the Chinghai-Tibet plateau, the team stops to perform for herdsmen and villagers. Dressed

PLA medics travel by camel.

in the gay holiday costume of the Tibetan peasants, the troupe does plays and dances with Communist themes. Sometimes it recites Mao Tsetung's sayings to music. After each show, the troupe helps the villagers and the herdsmen with their chores. The cultural team also collects folk songs and dances of these remote people.

The army tries to keep in close friendly contact with all the minority peoples who live in China. Most of these non-Chinese peoples live on the borders of China patrolled by PLA units. The minority people in the mountainous areas of southwestern China that border on Burma, Laos, and Vietnam are related to the peoples of those countries. The minority groups still speak their own language, dress in their own way, and follow their own customs. But they cooperate with the PLA and train for the People's Militia. Many of them are also being accepted into the army and are helping patrol their home areas which they know so well.

The Chinese government wants to establish better relationships with the minorities, so it grants membership in the Communist Party to some of them. Young Party members are then sent to the Central Institute for Nationalities in Peking. The institute was set up solely for minority pupils and houses seven hundred at a time They study Communism, the Chinese language, agriculture, animal breeding, and practical nursing.

When the young minority students return to their homes, they can use their new skills to help their own people. They also act as interpreters for the Chinese. As loyal *kan-pu* of the Communist Party, they win the trust of their own race in a way no outsider ever could do.

14

Resources

Forests are an important resource in almost every country. Unfortunately, those in China have been wasted by emperors and commoners alike.

In ancient times, the emperors used large quantities of lumber to build their magnificent wooden palaces. But in more modern times, it was the commoners who did the greatest damage. After the foreigners arrived in China, construction needs increased. The peasants found they could make a few cents' profit on each tree they delivered for lumber, so they cut them down in great numbers.

The peasants also discovered that corn and Irish potatoes introduced by the foreigners grew better in the cooler mountains. To prepare fields for these new crops, they burned down the forests that covered the steep slopes of mountains and hills. Without trees to hold the soil, the rains washed it away. This is known as erosion.

Each time the fields were washed away, the peasants moved on to clear new fields, increasing the danger of erosion. By the time the People's Republic of China was founded in 1949, there were very few trees left in the country.

The problem of erosion had become especially serious in the Great Loess. The soil is so fine that it can be carried off easily by wind or rain. The Chinese are now trying to anchor that soil in place by planting millions of trees on the hill and mountain slopes. But it is rather discouraging work because it is impossible to irrigate the trees, and many of them die in the dry season. Other trees are washed away before they can grow deep roots. The peasants, however, are always hopeful and patient, and go back to planting more.

The Chinese have had more success along China's border with Inner Mongolia and the Northeast Region (Manchuria). Here they have planted mile after mile of trees, reaching from the far western deserts to the Pacific Ocean in the east. Today a living green wall blocks the winds and shifting sands from the fields. The Chinese call it their Great Green Wall.

Tree planting has been going on everywhere else in China too. Young trees are now growing up the slopes of once barren mountains. On the plains, shade trees line canals, rivers, roads, and city streets. Large orchards of fruit and nut trees surround little villages. And along some sections of the coast, sturdy apple orchards block high sea gales and blowing sand from the fields to the east of them.

China still has a few natural forests left. They are in the remote mountains of the Northeast Region, southwest China, Tibet, and Fukien province. Forestry experts carefully regulate the lumber industry in these places, and new trees are planted whenever old ones have been cut down.

Salt, another of China's resources, comes from great salt lakes on the Chinghai-Tibet Plateau and deep wells in Szechuan. It is also made from evaporated sea water along the coast.

Deep sea fishing is important to China too. Fishing has

been carried on by the Chinese for centuries. In the old days, off the Fukien coast, families used to live aboard their junks. Food was cooked on deck over charcoal braziers. Beds were narrow compartments in the hold. Young children were tied to long ropes fastened to the mast to keep them from falling overboard. But they soon found their sea legs and became experienced sailors.

The great junks, with their patched sails billowing in the wind, are slow-moving and hard to handle. So the fishermen had to stay close to shore. Today fleets of modern trawlers, equipped with refrigerated holds and operated by the State, bring in huge catches. But the old-style sailing junk is still the most common boat on Chinese waters.

However, there have been changes. The fishermen, like the peasants, have formed communes and are pooling their resources. Gradually, they buy motorized junks or equip old sailing junks with motors which enable them to sail far out to sea. The junks, which also carry refrigeration equipment, work in pairs, hauling a large net between them. They come up with fine catches of yellow croakers, silvery hairtails, cuttlefish, and shrimp.

Far down south, in the Sisha Islands of the South China Sea, fishermen also trap lobsters, king sea slugs, and turtles, whose eggs they collect too. The catch either is sold fresh to the State or is dried, canned, or frozen in many processing plants along the coast. Much of this canned goods is exported to countries that have trade agreements with China. Among them are West Germany, Japan, and some Southeast Asia nations.

Freshwater fish are abundant too. Every pond, every canal, and even the ricefields are stocked with fish. Fleets of fishing sampans sail the lakes and rivers.

120

Sailing back after a good catch.

The rivers of China are important other than for fishing. For centuries they have been the country's chief means of transportation. In the far north the Heilung Kiang, or Black Dragon River, forms the boundary between the Northeast Region and Siberia. Large steamers sail back and forth from May to October when it is ice-free. In central China, the mighty Yangtze River, the most important means of transportation in all China, is open to large oceangoing freighters as far as Wuhan, 630 miles into the interior. Smaller river freighters can go as far as Chungking, on the other side of the Yangtze Gorges.

The Yellow River in the north and the short Si River in the south are too shallow for large ships. But they are alive with cargo barges, motor tugs, sampans, and junks, all carrying on a brisk traffic.

There is an odd thing about some of China's rivers. The land from Tibet in the west to the Pacific Ocean in the east tilts downward. Because of this, the main rivers run from west to east. But a network of navigable canals, cut from north to south, joins many of their tributaries. The longest is still the Grand Canal, which stretches from Hangchow in the south to Peking in the north.

Highways and railways help out with the transportation problem. Many new ones have been built since the founding of the People's Republic. Today it is possible to travel by rail from Peking to far western Sinkiang Province and from Kansu provice south to Yunnan. Two highways now connect once isolated Tibet with China. One runs east from Lhasa in Tibet to Szechuan province, and the other crosses the desolate Askai Chin plateau north into Sinkiang province.

More highways and railways are being built every year. But overland transportation is still a problem. For short distances the Chinese have to depend on donkeys, mules, horses, camels, and men to move goods from place to place.

New freighters, being built in China's own shipyards, sail the seas carrying cargoes to countries with which the People's Republic trades. China even has an airline service between her major cities, using planes purchased from other countries. And she is hoping to establish round-the-world passenger flights in the near future.

Some of China's underground resources have been known and used for years—the coal and iron in the Northeast Region, the coal in Shensi province, and the oil fields in Sinkiang province. In the old days, it was believed that China had far too few resources to sustain heavy industry. But after the People's Republic was founded, geologic teams were sent out by the government on exploration missions. They found rich new deposits of coal, iron ore, and minerals, such as tungsten, copper and manganese, all valuable to industry.

In 1958, geologic teams located large oil fields in the wild Tsaidam Basin in Chinghai province. Today the plain is studded with towering derricks. In 1962, rich oil deposits were discovered somewhere in China. The Chinese are keeping the location a secret, but it is probably in the Anta area near Harbin. Thousands of workers and their families were sent to develop the oil fields which were called Tachin, meaning "Great Celebration."

Tachin is an example of a new kind of industrial complex. Instead of one big congested city, it is made up of little villages where the oil workers and their families live. Each village is located near a work section and has its own shopping center, post office, clinic, and school. Each one is surrounded by fields, which are farmed by the families of the oil workers. The grain, vegetables, and livestock that they raise supply all the needs of each little settlement. This eliminates the necessity of transporting food in large quantities.

Many of the villages also have small factories, which are run by the wives of the workers. Using the waste materials from the oil fields, they make such by-products as industrial tar paper, soap, and chemical fertilizers.

Today the Chinese government is planning to create more of these industrial-agricultural complexes. As the new factories are built, the government will send skilled workers from the congested coastal areas to settle them. It hopes that, by putting the factories in the countryside, it will clean out the last crowded slum districts in the old cities.

The People's Republic of China has another important

reason for scattering her heavy industry. Ever since her quarrel with the Soviet Union became so bitter, she has been fearful of war. With her industrial complexes scattered, it will be almost impossible to bomb them all out, and China will therefore be able to carry on.

15

The Future

Twice a year, once in the spring and again in the fall, the People's Republic of China invites thousands of businessmen from all over the world to attend the Canton Fair in South China. The fair is an exhibit of China's many products. All the things shown represent the work of commune factories and the large industrial centers of the cities.

The products at the fair are displayed in showcases lining broad aisles. The list is endless—porcelain tea sets, clocks, watches, bicycles, sewing machines, radios, television sets, cameras, jade and ivory carvings, leather goods, steel tubing, high grade gasoline, high precision machine tools, farm tractors, grain, oils, cotton, silk, tobacco, fruit.

Transactions at the fair aren't made in a hurry. Long negotiations take place between the State representatives and the businessmen before the deals are set and the orders are drawn up. Especially important transactions require a trip to Peking and discussions with top government officials there.

China today is producing more goods than any other

country in Asia, but she is still very much underdeveloped. Long centuries of corrupt rule and more than one hundred and twenty-five years of foreign exploitation have made her poor. She has no large store of money from which to draw, and she doesn't like to borrow on credit.

Her steel output is expanding, but it must increase much more to fill all China's needs. Though agriculture is gradually becoming mechanized, a lot of farming is still being done by human beings and animals. Drought and flood still reduce the harvests. In recent years, China has had to buy wheat from Canada and the United States to provide enough for her people. She also is buying airplanes and heavy industry tools from other countries, including the Soviet Union.

China's closest economic relations today are with Japan. She has seen how Japan has built up a strong economy, so Chinese specialists are being sent to Japan to study their methods. With Japanese technology and help, China hopes to expand her own industries and eventually install nuclear power plants to overcome her power shortage.

The People's Republic looks forward to a future in which she will at last take her place as one of the great powers of the world. Already, she has surpassed many Western nations in the scientific field. She has sent a satellite to circle the earth, her first step in the exploration of space, in which she hopes to join the United States and the U.S.S.R. As part of her defense system, she is working on an intercontinental missile that, when armed with an atomic warhead, will go farther than those of other nations.

Yet over China's future stands one gigantic question mark. What will happen when death takes Chairman Mao Tsetung, who has held the country together? Will Premier Chou En-lai take his place? But the premier is seventy-five now only five years younger than Chairman Mao himself.

Recently, however, a new name is being heard more and more often—that of 38-year-old Wang Hung-wen. At the time of the Cultural Revolution, Mr. Wang was an unknown official at a Shanghai textile mill, but he rose rapidly in Communist Chinese circles. By 1973 when the Party held its Tenth Congress in Peking, he was introduced as the third ranking party official in the whole of China.

Today Wang is the only young man in the powerful nine-member Standing Committee of the Politburo. And he is given added importance by appearing with Mao whenever the Chairman receives important visitors such as President Pompidou of France.

The Western world wonders if Wang is being groomed to be Mao's successor. If so, as the next chairman of the Politburo, will this obscure young man be able to gain enough public backing to hold the country together?

If he fails, will China be ruled by a coalition group made up of members of the Politburo? Or will a man like Liu Shao-chi arise to take the country along the road of Russian-style revisionism which Mao Tsetung has been fighting against? Or will some other ambitious leader, hungry for power, try to turn China into a military dictatorship, using the army as Lin Piao tried to use it?

If no one proves strong enough to unite the country, will it again split into quarreling factions as it did during the Cultural Revolution? At that time only Chairman Mao's towering personality succeeded in pulling China together again. After he is gone, can Wang Hung-wen, or any other leader, prove strong and loyal enough to guide China along the way charted by Mao?

Only the future can tell.

Index